# The Vicar's Guide

# The Vicar's Guide

Life and ministry in the parish

edited by David Ison

 CHURCH HOUSE
PUBLISHING

Church House Publishing
Church House
Great Smith Street
London SW1P 3NZ

Tel: 020 7898 1451
Fax: 020 7898 1449

ISBN 0 7151 4015 9

Published 2005 by Church House Publishing

The opinions expressed in this book are those of
the individual authors and do not necessarily reflect
the official policy of the General Synod or The
Archbishops' Council of the Church of England.

Printed in England by The Cromwell Press,
Trowbridge, Wiltshire

# Contents

# About the authors

**David Ison** is Director of the Council for Worship and Ministry in Exeter Diocese, and a part-time canon at the cathedral.

**Stephen Conway** served in parochial ministry in the Diocese of Durham for sixteen years, at times combining working in parishes with other jobs like Director of Ordinands. He became the Archdeacon of Durham in 2002.

**Chris Edmondson** has been warden of the Lee Abbey Community and Conference Centre in North Devon since 2002 prior to which he has been in local parish or diocesan ministry since 1973.

**Sue Hope** spent seventeen years in parish ministry before becoming the Missioner for Sheffield Diocese. She is a Canon of Sheffield, and a Six Preacher of Canterbury Cathedral.

**Felicity Lawson** has been a parish worker, theological college lecturer, diocesan director of ministerial training, director of ordinands and is now Vicar of Gildersome in the Wakefield Diocese.

**Roger Morris** is the Director of the Forum for Parish Development and Evangelism in the Diocese of Coventry. Before taking up this role, he spent seven years as the Rector of nine rural churches in Gloucestershire.

**Ann Morisy** has a worked with many local churches helping them to think through their involvement with the wider community. She has given a lot of thought to how social action and mission can be inter-related. She is the Director of the Commission on Urban Life and Faith.

**Philip North** is the Priest Administrator of the Shrine of Our Lady of Walsingham. Prior to that he spent ten years in the Diocese of Durham serving in parishes in Sunderland and Hartlepool. He is a member of the Church of England's College of Evangelists.

**Anne Richards** is Mission Theology Adviser to the Mission and Public Affairs department of the Archbishops' Council and Secretary of the ecumenical Mission Theological Advisory Group.

**David Runcorn** is Director of Ministry Development in Lichfield Diocese. Prior to this he was a vicar in West London before becoming Director of Pastoral Studies, Evangelism and tutor in Spirituality at Trinity Theological College in Bristol.

**Darren Smith** has for the past thirteen years been the Parish Priest of St Luke's, Kingstanding in the Diocese of Birmingham.

**Guy Wilkinson** has served in a wide variety of parishes in Coventry, Guildford and Birmingham dioceses and until 2004 as Archdeacon of Bradford. He now works on resourcing urban churches with Anthony Collins Solicitors and with the Mission and Public Affairs department of the Archbishops' Council.

**Stephen Wright** is Director of the College of Preachers, an ecumenical training and support network, and an associate lecturer at Spurgeon's College, London.

**Jennifer Zarek** has been vicar of four rural parishes in Yorkshire for the past five years.

# Introduction

The way in which it happens will be different, but the realization is the same:
I have the responsibility for sorting this out. The curacy or training post is over
and whether it is the awkward question, the heated argument, or the dispute
about policy, the buck has arrived on the desk. Shared ministry notwithstanding,
it is the ordained person whom everybody is looking at; and, especially for the
first time, it can be an alarming and uncomfortable feeling.

The needs which have given rise to this book are those expressed by ministers
in their 'post of first responsibility'. The contributors have written out of their own
experience: primarily with Anglican parish clergy, 'vicars', in mind, but also aware
of other colleagues in ministry. There is much here that will speak to ministers of
churches across all traditions, and to Anglicans and others whose responsibilities
are exercised in chaplaincy, mission or secular employment, full- or part-time.

Over the centuries there has been a venerable tradition of books to help the
clergy, from Gregory the Great's sixth-century *Book of Pastoral Rule*, through
George Herbert's *The Country Parson* and Percy Dearmer's *The Parson's Handbook*
to contemporary books on church management, legal requirements and pastoral
care. This book is a little different, for two reasons. The first is that it stresses the
need to understand and engage with the context in which ministry is set. The
pace of social and economic change is rather faster than in George Herbert's
day, faster even than the processes of industrialization and the accompanying
professionalism which to a relatively limited extent affected the working patterns
and aspirations of clergy during the nineteenth and twentieth centuries. For
example, telephones, email and entry-phones, the breakdown of traditional
community and a loss of social status for ministers of religion have all changed
expectations about visiting on both sides of the doorstep, to differing extents in
differing places, valuable as visiting people at home will always be. There is no
single right way any more (if there ever was) in which to be a vicar: but there
are more or less appropriate ways in given contexts, and this book will help
you explore those ways.

The second difference is that the focus throughout is not so much on the work
to be done – though there is plenty said about that – but on resourcing the
minister to be able to do that work. This is not, however, an individualistic
exercise. Now, more than ever, there is a proper awareness of how responsibility
for ministry is shared. It is still the case that legal structures as well as popular
expectations encourage the idea that there is a leader who will 'sort it all out',

and that the parish priest is that leader. Having the personal resources to deal creatively with the pressure, or temptation, to have the answer for everything, and to be a leader who enables others, is of crucial importance for the health of the minister as well as the Church.

So the book begins by looking at changes in context and role, and then at the resources available to parish clergy. It turns to look in more detail at how to cope personally and spiritually with the demands of parish ministry: who are you called to become? It then tackles the overall question of vision – what are you called to do? – and applies this to the central task of mission. The responsibility of 'running a church' effectively in order to pursue mission is explored, including the need for good leadership shared within a church. Different aspects of the context in which ministry is set are then discussed, before looking more specifically at the tasks of preaching and worship as ways in which to express the calling of church and minister. Two appendices offer further resources on working in the parish and gaining more information about the context of ministry.

Whether you find receiving the buck exciting, daunting, stressful or fulfilling, there have been many others who have gone before you, and their experience is there to help and sustain you. The authors of this book hope that you will be encouraged along your journey of ministry in the company of all God's people, so that 'all of us come to the unity of the faith and of the knowledge of the Son of God, to maturity, to the measure of the full stature of Christ'.

*David Ison*

# I

# The changing role of the vicar

Guy Wilkinson

By contrast with their professional counterparts in the secular world, most parish clergy are only now beginning to enter the changed world that most other professions have lived in for a decade. Ask a member of a congregation, someone in the high street and a vicar a generation ago and now, what the clergy do and their answers now would be recognizably in continuity with the answers they gave then. True, she now was a he then; there are fewer now than then and spread across more congregations; there is less visiting now; more paperwork, more emails, more informality. But vicars still live in vicarages, lead services in churches, chair their PCCs, conduct funerals, weddings and baptisms, are on the governing bodies of their Church schools and take an active part in the wider life of the community. We are still virtually guaranteed a monthly stipend and housing through to retirement with a non-contributory pension. The Church of England has retained a universal presence, particularly in the urban areas where other denominations have not found this possible, and the structure of the parochial system remains intact (albeit very stretched) through the devices of groups, teams, clusters and other ways of reallocating a slowly reducing resource of stipendiary clergy.

## Change and evolution

Changes in society around us are increasingly calling forth pressures for change from within the Church as it reaches the limits of what can be achieved by reorganization of the basic parochial model. Increasingly there will be a premium for those dioceses and individual churches that enable clergy to connect more with the lived experience of the wider population, that rely less on simply stretching clergy to cover more of the same, and that offer ways which are more provisional and responsive to the times. This does not necessarily mean that the Church of England must withdraw from its historic role on the ground, nor that the role of 'vicar' must give way to something unrecognizably different. It does, however, mean that clergy will need to work within an environment in which their ministry is more varied, less secure and more open-ended than it has been for a very long time.

# Continuing change and evolution

Uncomfortable though it might be to be called to minister in a time of transition, we have no particular 'right' to remain in the mould in which we were formed. Nor can it really be argued that the present model of parish ministry is the only true model, the zenith of what has gone before. Through the centuries there have been many changes and the story which has brought us to the vicar of today is a long one beginning with something very different. The early 'frontier' days, through the medieval world of Chaucer's parson and nun's priest, through the Reformation and down to the rationalist days of the earlier eighteenth century – all these gave way eventually in the nineteenth century to new forms of urban, social and political engagement and to the professionalization of the clergy as the foundation of the role in which we find ourselves to be today. There has been much that has changed and it is important to keep a sense of perspective and to accept that much more change may be in store.

We have over the past decade seen some changes, comparatively modest though they may have been. Women have been ordained for a decade now and they, just as men, are being ordained later in life, often bringing significant previous experience with them and often formed by wider society in ways that will not have been true for earlier generations. There are and, for at least a time to come, will continue to be fewer stipendiary clergy but as part of an increasingly diverse and untidy range of authorized ministries, ordained and lay. Clergy will have less continuous patterns of employment as the range and type of ministries increase and we shall have to learn more about what it is to be seen as partners in ministry rather than primarily as the leaders of the Christian community.

Some changes are worth noting in more detail as they may well be the harbingers of some of the further changes to come, particularly if the intention is to remain within the frameworks of the professions.

# Appointments

The appointment processes for parish clergy have begun to change markedly and largely under the pressure of the changes experienced for a considerable time by lay members of the congregations in their own professional working lives. Concepts of equal opportunity have been the foundation and upon them the human resource managers have built a plethora of techniques aimed at assessing candidates against each other in competitive contexts. It is not only about assessing skills and abilities, but also the extent to which a candidate for a post will fit the team or corporate culture, the need for particular skills and experience and the personality that a candidate brings to an appointment. This is the approach that is increasingly infiltrating the world of appointments to parish posts and which has been facilitated by changes in the Benefices Measure to provide more opportunity for parish representatives to have their voice heard and respected by patrons. The days in which a country patron might advertise in *Horse and Hound* and appoint at his sole discretion are gone and the days when it is considered acceptable for a bishop or other patron simply to appoint over the heads of the parish, are fast disappearing. Much more frequently, posts are advertised, standard application forms and appointment processes are agreed, and appointment panels with training in interview techniques are constituted. Decisions are now more often arrived at on the basis of the consensus view of the panel and then accepted by patron and bishop. Of course headhunting of particular people for particular posts remains both in the secular world and in the Church, but there is a developing culture in which such approaches are treated with suspicion and require clear justification.

This approach challenges both the entrenched introversion of the patronage system and also the clergy who have had long experience of a quite different way of appointment, one in which they have looked to their bishop to indicate when and in what direction, or to which parish their next move should be. To have to apply for an advertised post and to market oneself as the best person for the appointment goes deeply against the grain of a tradition which, at its best, emphasizes self-effacement and servanthood but at its worst encourages dependency and mediocrity. This will continue to be a further profound challenge for the Church, both for clergy and for lay people involved in the making of appointments to parishes. Can a closed appointment process be reconciled with an acceptance of equal opportunities and the competitive spirit and with a desire to discern the mind of the Holy Spirit? To this must also be added the proper desire of the Church to be pastorally concerned to support those who in this more rugged and worldly approach may not easily be appointed. How can those who, with their families, have given their lives to the Church, be discounted or discarded because no parish in the diocese measures them well against other candidates?

## Employment contracts

If the appointment processes are changing, then so are the terms on which clergy hold office. For many generations, the normal expectation has been for the vicar to be appointed to the living as incumbent with the freehold, a concept rooted in property ownership and exercised through a complex of patronage rights. The freehold provided security of tenure, initially for a lifetime and more recently through to retirement at an upper limit of 70. The concept of freehold is now under real pressure with up to one third of all clergy ministering under some form of more time-limited arrangement.[1] Some see the freehold as an essential defence for the freedom of the parish clergy against unreasonable diktat by bishops or by factions within the congregation. Others see it as a level of security beyond that experienced by most of their parishioners and inconsistent with their Lord who had no place to lay his head. Perhaps at least it may be said that for every advantage of freedom to exercise a ministry under God without undue interference or pressure from particular factions or from bishops and archdeacons, there is a corresponding disadvantage: lack of accountability, a privileging of individuality over and against the corporate interest and a risk of the loss of the freshness and edge that pastoral and prophetic ministry both require.

Clergy in the Church of England receive their authority to minister from the bishop by institution to a benefice, by licence or by a written permission to officiate. Institution to a freehold has increasingly given way to various forms of licensed ministry as team ministries have grown in number across the country. Seven-year contracts for team vicars and increasingly for team rectors, less formal arrangements for priests in charge where presentation to a living has been suspended, and a wide variety of chaplaincy arrangements have all combined to give a situation where nearly 40 per cent of all clergy hold their ministry on the basis of a licence without freehold or employment contract. Underlying this situation has been the self-employed status of clergy which, apart from a short period in the 1960s, has been maintained. The legal fiction that clergy are not employed by a bishop, a diocese or the Church of England, but are licensed office holders has been retained.

Once again it is the forces external to the Church that are leading to changes to this diverse set of arrangements which had grown haphazardly over the years. At one end of the spectrum almost complete lifetime security; at the other the possibility of licence being summarily revoked by a bishop without further processes. The source of external pressure has rather surprisingly been the Department of Trade and Industry which has sought to provide additional employment rights to people who are not technically employees. Some order may be brought to the employment arrangements for clergy by the range of proposals brought to Synod in early 2004 which include the concept of 'common tenure', the provision of a variety of terms of service, access to Employment Tribunals to appeal, among other things, against unfair dismissal and a variety of accountability and capability procedures. All of these things tend to move the clergy further towards the same frames of reference that other professionals have operated within for some time.

## Review, evaluation and performance assessment

Ministerial review in one form or another has become an established process across all dioceses in the past ten years and at its best is largely accepted as a proper way, not simply of providing accountability, but of a process of mutual discernment, correction and encouragement which should normally characterize Christian relationships. Of course, unlike in the secular world, there are no material sanctions or rewards available to be applied and it might be hoped that this is seen as a positive aspect which respects the fundamental collegiality of clergy, including those who are area deans, archdeacons or bishops. The advent of a new basis for disciplinary procedures in the Clergy Discipline Measure 2003 and the proposals for formal capability procedures made in 2004 by the review group chaired by Professor David McClean may, however, introduce a quite different edge to ministerial review in the future.[2]

But additional pressures towards accountability are also coming to the Church as well as to the wider world, and with the slow but steadily reducing numbers attending church on Sundays and with increasing financial pressures, performance targets are at least implicitly becoming part of the armoury of management techniques that dioceses are bringing to bear. These pressures are exacerbated by the limited methods of measuring the healthiness of a church and the reliance upon Electoral Roll and Usual Sunday Attendance figures. Since these are normally the basis of share or common fund calculations, they come to have the status of performance targets. Clergy can be squeezed both by the wider diocesan systems, which increasingly look to parishes to contribute at least the cost of providing them with a priest; and by the PCC which is encouraged by such an approach to see the vicar as 'theirs'– the one whom they have paid for and by extension whom they employ. In some dioceses the tensions have been exacerbated by calculations of the viability of parishes as measured by a series of numerical factors which are then used to determine whether a parish shall continue to have stipendiary clergy. In other dioceses some larger parishes that contribute significantly more than the costs of their own clergy to the common funds are tempted to use this as a lever in support of their own particular perspectives.

## Individualism and partnership

These tendencies make for very difficult contexts for clergy to minister in and threaten to undermine the basis of the Church as able to minister in all localities irrespective of their financial strength. The context will be increasingly difficult the more clergy seek to hold on to the concept of the parson – the person – in his or her parish ministering as the omnicompetent leader of the Christian community and often in the wider parish community as well. The development of groups and even teams has not yet delivered a sufficient change to the underlying culture of an essentially individual clerical leadership – albeit supported by churchwardens, Readers and the PCC more generally – that had been hoped for. The emphasis on collaborative ministry within the life of the local church and between neighbouring churches is widespread and there is also a growing emphasis on partnership working between the Church and other agencies, particularly in urban contexts. There is, however, still a long way to travel in this direction as PCCs and congregations are not always supportive, preferring as often as not, to hold on to the deeply rooted, centuries-old tradition of 'our vicar'. But the change is coming and the development of new patterns of team working based on specialism and complementarity will become the norm among the coming generation of clergy. Patterns will be more complex with, for example, local ministry teams drawing together a wide variety of specialist paid lay ministries, stipendiary and self-supporting clergy, and a variety of voluntary ministries. These changes will call for quite different patterns of skills and attitudes than we have for the most part been used to and will be challenging for clergy and lay Christians alike.

As stipendiary clergy become fewer, and as the range of authorized lay and ordained ministries increases, there are real questions about the core role within a parish, team or area that they should play. Many of the ministerial tasks that have been associated with the vicar can quite appropriately be undertaken by lay ministers, and for the vicar to hold on to them increasingly gives rise to questions about the exercise of power. Presidency at the Eucharist provides a natural foundation for a wider leadership in the Church – albeit a servant leadership and one undertaken in a wider corporate context – and 'vicars' will increasingly find themselves called to the roles of leadership and management that their peers in other professions have long since been called to undertake. Once again there is a challenge to pastoral and 'chaplaincy' models that will not be resolved easily. But there is also a challenge to the prevailing assumption that the only alternative is the professional model.

## What does the future look like?

The future for clergy will, in part, lie in the direction of greater diversity, more provisionality and less security but with a countervailing tendency towards more training, clearer contractual and employment status, greater inclusion within formal managerial systems and greater accountability.

This will be a continuing story for clergy, one in which the Church nationally will struggle to find ways in which it can manage an often competing set of forces. It will need to continue to seek a framework within which clergy have a degree of security appropriate to their ministry in the institution which in all but the formal sense employs them. It will also continue to want to respect the individual vocation and freedom under the Holy Spirit. The wider culture places its emphasis on an individualistic approach to rights more than it does on corporate responsibilities. The Church brings, or should bring, an appreciation of grace over law, a strong understanding of covenant over contract, a high understanding of vocation and a concern for the dignity of its ministers under God.

These are complex and important matters on which the well-being of many clergy and their families will continue to be built and which will require an unravelling of much that has been inherited. The test for the Church will be whether it is possible to develop patterns of mutuality in ministry and vocation that are more true to the covenant relationship between God and humanity than they are to western legal and civic constructs.

It is not difficult to understand from this overview that the context into which men and women will increasingly be ordained to minister in parishes is likely to be quite different from that of a generation ago. The Ordinal may not change greatly in its description of what priests are called to. Indeed, the role of the vicar as one sharing in responsibility for the 'cure of souls' in a neighbourhood may remain largely as it is at present. What is changing – and will change further – is the institutional framework within which such ministry is to be undertaken and, in particular, the extent to which clergy and their churches will feel free to minister in ways that correspond to the changing realities of their contexts. There is a real challenge for dioceses to find ways to avoid becoming just another institutional corporate employer, albeit ecclesiastical rather than secular.

A secular organization relies on being able to retain and motivate its people by rewards and sanctions, by the quality of its products and by the nature of its corporate culture. The Church is not so different that these things are irrelevant to it, but it is different in that its clergy and lay people draw their foundational inspiration and motivation not from the Church as organization, but from the person of Jesus and the inspiration of the Holy Spirit. The task for the Church in relation to clergy is to enable them to live out their inspiration in the local contexts in which they minister together with others.

An important part of this enabling will be a renewed attention to patterns of continuing training and development with an emphasis not just on new technical skills, but much more on ways of working in relationship, on listening, discerning and communicating and on understanding and taking forward the heart of what it is to be an ordained person in a kaleidoscopic, postmodern, western world.

Inevitably it will not be possible for all clergy to respond comfortably to all these changes. For some the changes will be welcome and offer a much greater set of opportunities to explore different modes of being responsible for the care of souls. For others, change will be hugely significant in that they will find themselves at a loss and feel that they are strangers in their own home, with the attendant risks of ending their ministry in disillusion and even bitterness. This will not always be something that can be addressed effectively by training since it is a matter of culture and formation much more than it is of specific skills. At present the Church has rather few means to address such situations and needs quite urgently to acquire ways in which some can step back from full parish responsibilities into forms of early retirement, part-time or flexible patterns of working or indeed the possibility of retaining earnings from specialist skills.

Where are all these changes leading? Is it the case, as many fear, that clergy are destined to become little more than managers in the local Christian community, holding together a disparate team of lay and ordained colleagues? Or will they be sidelined as local specialists in prayer and the leading of worship, or perhaps employees of the corporate Church at the beck and call of diocesan managers and autocratic bishops? Perhaps many will in one way or another continue to be the vicar who cares for the souls of local people and has the courage and humility to follow a vocation that will continue to be little understood but widely valued.

What lies ahead for clergy and their roles will be exciting and fulfilling for those who are ready and equipped, but will create anxiety and hardship for those who are not. The heart of the role will remain what it has always been – a person called by God and authorized by the Church to be at the heart of a local Christian community. To lead in prayer and sacrament, to interpret, to initiate, to pastor and to enable others to do these things is a great privilege.

# 2

# Continuing training

David Ison

> In a higher world it is otherwise, but here below to live is to change, and to be perfect is to have changed often.[1]

There is a section in the standard Church of England application form headed 'Continuing Ministerial Education' (CME), which asks the applicant to list training courses attended. There is a good reason for this: if ministers want to learn and are open to growth, then they are more likely to develop a growing and lively church. But asking this question – indeed, having an application form for parish posts at all – would have been unthinkable a generation ago. Things have moved on since 1980 when the General Synod paper *The Continuing Education of the Church's Ministers* was published, CME began to develop a clear structure and purpose in the Church of England, and the Inland Revenue increasingly acknowledged that a well-equipped priest would require rather more resources than just a Bible and a *Book of Common Prayer* for the duration of their ministry.

## What's it all about?

Ministers have always been expected to learn – or rather, be learned. There has been a clear understanding that studying theology is a normal part of ministerial life, and not only in order to prepare sermons. But, as the question on the application form indicates, there is now a public and accountable dimension to this learning, and specialist assistance is provided to enable appropriate education throughout the whole of a person's ministry. Why is this so?

The report *Mind the Gap* published in 2001 sets out a number of reasons for this development. Two are of particular importance: the first is that 'the past twenty years have witnessed a rapid strengthening of the conviction that one of the primary tasks of the clergy and other accredited ministers is to evoke ministry and mission among the whole people of God.'[2] In other words, ministers have to enable other people to learn and grow in ministry; and how can we do that for them if we're not doing it ourselves? If we are building a Church in which people are continually learning about their faith and ministry, in the setting of a world in which life-long learning is seen as important, we too must go on learning, pursuing the Pauline vision of growing into 'the measure of the full stature of Christ' (Ephesians 4.13).

The second reason for the higher profile of CME is that the world is changing rapidly, and the Church struggles to keep in touch with it. No longer will initial training equip you for every eventuality. When I was ordained in inner-city London in 1979, manual typewriters were the order of the day, and photocopiers were unattainably expensive; telephones were only just essential; personal computers, mobile phones, email and the Internet were science fiction; there were no child protection procedures that we knew about, health and safety was for industry not churches, and we happily entertained 'gentlemen of the road' in our own homes. At least I was familiar with services in modern language, although I hadn't noticed that women weren't included in them. Looking ahead, where will your ministry and mine be by the year 2025? If we don't learn and change, then our ministry – and the gospel we have to share – will be seen as increasingly old-fashioned and irrelevant. As the Declaration of Assent made by Church of England clergy at their licensing puts it, we 'profess the faith uniquely revealed in the Holy Scriptures and set forth in the catholic creeds, *which faith the Church is called upon to proclaim afresh in each generation* ... will you affirm your loyalty to this inheritance ... in bringing the grace and truth of Christ to this generation ...?' This is a worthy sentiment; but what resources does the minister need in order to make this proclamation a reality?

## What does it cover?

When ministers first get ordained, it isn't uncommon for them to sigh with relief at the thought that training is 'really' over, and get stuck into the practical business of ministry. Post-ordination training (POT – also known as CME 1–4, or in future as Initial Ministerial Education 4–6) has often been seen as something that competes with real ministry, rather than as a means of enhancing it. During a healthy initial training post, however, ministers should be learning how to integrate what they already know – from past work and life experience as well as pre-ordination training – with the real questions people ask and the needs that they have, and begin to recognize their own questions and needs for further learning and development.

The landlord of the local pub had died, and I went to see his widow after the funeral for a follow-up pastoral visit. I thought I was being sympathetic and understanding, till she said to me, 'You're trying to make me cry, aren't you?' She was a private person who wanted to grieve in her way, not mine. Her honesty provoked me to reassess my pastoral practice and my ideas about grieving. I went to learn from a widowed curate in the next-door parish, whom I then assisted in running a bereavement course for people in the local community.

The move from curacy to post of first responsibility, sometimes anticipated by a period of running a vacancy, highlights the three areas of ministry in which we need to continue developing and learning:

## Skills: how we do things, and do them well

Moving provokes an immediate rash of practical questions, most of which you won't be aware of until they arise. How do you do it *here*, what are the procedures for *that*, is it legal, what happens when, and why do I have to do that? You need ways of finding answers to these questions, like having a hotline to colleagues within and outside your area of responsibility (churchwarden, secretary, rural dean, etc. – or possibly your former training incumbent). You will also need to work more generally on areas where you are less strong, and not avoid them: what do you find challenging? And in a work setting where you are often working on your own, with little formal provision for feedback: how can you consolidate skills, and how can you discover where your ministerial practice is not really good enough? It's much easier to assume we do something well than take the trouble to find out and change: and because they receive little positive affirmation, ministers are often afraid of constructive criticism and vulnerability, and tend to compete with one another.

Tony was chatting to the funeral director at the crem. 'Most ministers seem to think they do a great job,' she said, 'but they don't. You'd be horrified at the way many of them behave when they take funerals, and in dealing with bereaved people.' Tony was challenged by that, and talked with the CME officer in the diocese: this led to several sessions where funeral directors met with local ministers to talk about good practice and expectations. Tony tried to get a fellow minister from another church to sit in on a funeral that he led and give feedback afterwards, but none of them was willing, so he got someone from his church to do it instead.

## Knowledge: how we understand and interpret

What are we trying to do here? Where is God at work? How does this relate to what goes on elsewhere in the world and the Church? How can theology and practice go together? Society moves on and develops, as do theology and church life. If your theology qualification is over five years old, it's outdated. That doesn't mean that all your theology is outdated, but rather that you need to keep in touch with cultural and theological changes in order to continue the task of 'bringing the grace and truth of Christ to this generation'.

## Personal development: how we pray and grow as individuals

If the gospel isn't good news for you, it won't be good news for anyone. Growing in discipleship is our primary calling, upon which ministry depends: baptism comes before ordination. Understanding how you work, becoming aware of the hurts and sins you carry around and how they damage your relationships with God and others, and addressing them before God, are a crucial part of continuing your ministerial education. Many ministries have come to grief through the unwillingness of clergy to be self-aware and open to personal challenge and change.

# What do I do?

Most posts have some kind of ministerial review, which normally includes a question around what in-service training and support would be helpful, with information being sent to the CME Officer. If your post doesn't have this, then make it happen! It's an important way of gaining support and encouragement: so ask someone you can trust to help you identify your needs and priorities for further education and training. One way of doing this is to make a note of times that you feel the need for more understanding, skills or support. Another is to work through lists of expectations about the competence and ministry of ordained ministers (such as the Ordinal, lists of competencies for ministers such as those in the Ministry Division document *Beginning Public Ministry*, or the list of expectations in *Mind the Gap*.[3] A further way is to use open questions such as:

- What are the things that give you most joy and satisfaction in your life and ministry?

- What are the things that concern or worry you most in your life and ministry?

- What do you feel about the way in which you work? What is good about it, and what is difficult?

- How well does your work enable you to use and develop your abilities? What do you enjoy doing? What do you feel less confident about, or dislike doing? Are there strengths that need developing and/or weaknesses you need to work on?

- How much of your work can and should be shared with others?

- How well does your work meet the expectations of others and of yourself? Are those expectations reasonable?

- How could you change your pattern of life and ministry to make more use of the opportunities available to you?

- How balanced is your physical, mental, emotional and spiritual health, and what could you do to resource it better?

Once you have identified what you need, you then have to consider the best ways of meeting those needs: it isn't possible to do it all at once! Also, a balanced approach will help you develop most fully: rather than going on the same preaching conference every year, aim to do something different each year to resource your understanding, skills and personal growth. *Mind the Gap*[4] includes a framework to help the minister assess how broad their development is. It lays out as a graph the three dimensions of being a minister – personal, local to your post, the wider Church and world – against three directions in CME – interpreting the Christian tradition, forming church life, and addressing situations in the world – and invites you to locate your training needs on the graph to see how training resources are being allocated. This may highlight areas where more time and energy needs to be invested in training.

---

**Nigel phoned me up to talk about CME. He hadn't done any for a few years, and was wondering what to do. I went to see him, and after talking through his situation we agreed that he needed to come on a prison chaplaincy course to develop his awareness of that ministry; he should find a local computer course to develop his skills; and that he should take up fly fishing.**

---

# Where do I go?

Having identified their learning needs, how do ministers find relevant CME? There are various kinds of provision: your CME officer is there to act as an adviser and reference point for what is available and how to access it, and it's well worth consulting them about it. Many ministers sort out their own programmes, often using diocesan or district schemes for delivery and financial support. The main avenues are:

## Local

A surprising amount of relevant CME can be found locally. This may be through informal contacts such as the sharing of experience through a chapter or fraternal, or talking with ordained and lay colleagues over a cup of coffee. Specialist ministers are usually delighted to be invited to share ideas with a local meeting, which may not be able to attract speakers of national calibre, but which will gain in relevance since topics can be related to the immediate local context. There are also formal ways of learning locally: the local Council for Voluntary Service, adult education centre and FE college will run relevant courses, e.g. in information and communication technology, managing volunteers or counselling: learning opportunities are not restricted to church contexts.

## Diocese/district/region

Nearly all denominations have annual programmes of CME available, with a designated CME Officer to assist clergy in developing their ministry. There are usually grant schemes available to help with the cost of events, which can include seminars, day conferences, courses and residentials, covering all kinds of topics from the latest New Testament theology to time management. There should be some specialist courses for those in different kinds of ministry, including the first post of responsibility after training – so look out for these.

## National

There is a wide array of agencies offering all kinds of courses, with brochures and adverts in magazines, the church press and the Internet. From Bible Society to the Mennonites, from Praxis for worship to the Grubb Institute for leadership, there are many bodies that promote educational opportunities linked to their specialism (including an occasional Church Pastoral Aid Society conference for those in first incumbency). CME Officers should be able to give advice about these possibilities, which can vary in value and in intended clientele, and how they relate to other provision. There are also many societies that have national conferences which offer CME opportunities.

## Academic

For theological development, there are universities with theological or religious studies departments and libraries, which a minister can attend as an associate student, and which often have open lectures, extra-mural departments and seasonal schools (Oxford has one) – but beware of summer prices aimed at visiting American scholars. Church HE colleges, theological colleges past and present, and missionary colleges may offer courses in aspects of theology, culture and church life. Distance learning is another route, although this needs approaching with care as some providers are better than others; the Lambeth Diploma and MA is a cost-effective and flexible route. There are also cathedral or bishop's lectures or equivalent, which can provide easy access to leading scholars.

## Sabbaticals

Most dioceses have some sort of provision for sabbaticals, though not often as generous as the Methodist and URC schemes. A sabbatical is a period (normally of three months) for rest and refreshment, not for hard-working study leave. It should include a balance of physical, mental and spiritual re-creation, away from the everyday pressures of ordinary ministry. People undertake an enormous range of things, from studying or exchanging overseas to building a kit car! Requirements may vary, but sabbaticals should be planned in conjunction with the bishop or CME officer, and should be seen to be meeting the agreed needs of the minister concerned.

---

James had been ordained and in parish ministry for 20 years without a break, and was feeling tired and overstretched. After discussion with the CME officer, he planned a sabbatical which included: a major clergy conference, an eight-day retreat, a ten-day pilgrimage walk round the coast path, classes in woodworking and building a wardrobe, a holiday in Europe and a theological reading project.

---

# Things to bear in mind

When planning a personal CME programme, it's worth thinking about the following issues:

- Resource limitations. Courses cost money, including the fares to get there; they also cost time and energy, not only in being there, but in preparing to go and clearing up afterwards. You need to be realistic about what you and others around you can undertake.

- Accountability. CME is not a personal indulgence (although some church people see it as such): it's there to help ministers work better, in the broadest sense. To whom do you need to give an account of what you do? It's worth involving churchwardens/church council/elders and other leaders in planning what you do, so that they will support it and see it as part of what you do with them in ministry.

- Professional or personal? Ministers are required to be trained in certain things and ensure that they are done properly, such as child protection or filling in registers. Some training is required for professional development. But ministers also need to do things that will be satisfying and stretching, which have an element of fun and challenge. Neither full regulation nor total consumer choice are adequate models for a balanced CME provision.

- Career development. Very few ministers are appointed to 'senior posts', but all ministers have a career in ministry. God is calling you to have a unique place in the ministry of the Church: no one else will have your gifts and experience, and you are called to grow and develop them. Never do anything simply because you think you will 'get on' if you do it – that's a recipe for frustration and disappointment. But you should seek to develop your strengths as well as work on your weaknesses, in order to offer your gifts appropriately. All ministers have a specialism to offer the Church: what's your particular interest and passion? How can you foster and use it, whether or not it's the basis for a move in future? It's a gift from God – don't waste it.

## Taking responsibility for yourself

Structures of employment for ministers puzzle most people inside and outside the churches. The bottom line is that those of us who are ministers are responsible for our own support structures. There are resources available to help, through CME, ministry review, consultancy, pastoral care, etc.; but it is up to us to ask for and make use of them. The most important single thing to do when beginning a new post is to get the support structure sorted out, and change it as required: without that, it is difficult to survive the long-term pressures of ministry. The following elements should be included in a support package, however they are made up and recombined:

### To share with others

'It is not good for humans to be alone.' Jesus sent out his disciples in pairs, not as lone rangers. Chapters, fraternals and team meetings are structured places to share together, if they actually operate as they should. If they don't, work to change them and make them worth while. When I was a new vicar in a large deanery, the staff in the parishes on either side met every Monday morning for prayer and coffee and letting it all hang out. It was a real life-saver!

Don't collude in being nice, or competitive with each other – ministers need to develop a culture of reality and mutual support. Even Jesus' disciples had their group relationship problems.

## To be alone

Introverts can find groups overwhelming; extroverts can find silence threatening. But all of us need to make silence and space for God – which is why an annual silent retreat lasting at least three days is encouraged for all ministers. Going to a conference is simply not the same. If it's difficult to get away, have a quarterly quiet day; if there isn't an obvious place to go nearby, see if a church member will make their house available while they are out at work.

## To reflect confidentially

We need others to reflect back to us how we're getting on and what we are thinking. We may also need someone to help us take responsibility for difficult decisions and pastoral issues. This need can be met through a consultant, a life coach, a supervisor/counsellor, even a cell group or friend who is willing to challenge when required. There are times when we will require help to understand what's really going on.

## To be accountable

This is not meant in a heavy sense, but realistically. 'I'm accountable only to God' means that I account to no one, not even God. How do ministers live out their accountability? We need others to represent God to us, as we help others encounter God. A spiritual director, soul friend, and/or ministerial reviewer should have permission to stretch and confront us, for our own good before God.

## To learn

Learning comes not just through CME, but in taking time to be reflective and creative with what CME may give us. Ministers who don't read, think, listen and learn soon run out of spiritual life. We should look for ways to receive feedback on what we do, and learn from it.

*To be loved and accepted, with our mistakes and failings*

Taking time to nurture friendships which can give unconditional acceptance is an important part of setting up ministerial support. Ministers must not make the mistake of being too busy to have friends – they'll need them.

## To be renewed

Everyone needs a sense of identity in order to be able to be secure enough to give to others. Clustering together with those of like mind in regular conferences, cell groups or elsewhere can reinforce our identity. This can be helpful, but it can also get in the way of spiritual growth and breadth in ministry. Ministers need both to work at a positive sense of their identity, and to be prepared to lose it as God calls them on to new things. Are we stuck in an identity that excludes others and means we don't feel we can change without losing our friends? Do we ever go out to meet people who are different from us, who may even make us feel threatened? If not, why not? To fear and block change is to fail to live out the calling to share the gospel with everyone, everywhere, at all times.

Continuing Ministerial Education offers an opportunity to grow. What are we waiting for?

## For further reading

*Beginning Public Ministry*, ABM Ministry Paper 17, Church House Publishing, 1998.

*Mind the Gap: Integrated Continuing Ministerial Education for the Church's Ministers*, The Archbishops' Council, Church House Publishing, 2001.

# 3

# Self-management

David Runcorn

## Taking care of yourself

What would you expect to be included in this chapter? Probably a selection from that familiar litany of exhortations to healthy lifestyle, exercise and time off in busy ministry? You know the kind of thing. By the last page (if it works) you will be regularly walking/jogging/playing squash/other ... and have switched back to margarine. You will be hacking through the jungle of your diary to make a clearing for a rare evening out with your nearest and dearest; and waiting with nervous excitement to try out your newly found assertive side. A firm 'no!' awaits the next unsuspecting church member who calls you to ask for something on your day off. Oh and where did I put the leaflet about the Leisure Centre I picked up last year, to book that lunch-time aerobics class?

Of course these things are important. But it is no use talking as if there is a blueprint available that guarantees healthy ministers. If it was quite so easy we would have all been doing this a long time ago. As it is my own ministry history is littered with wrecks of schemes that never quite became the transforming habits I hoped for, including the obligatory exercise bike in the spare bedroom, which (along with most of the adult population) I sold, virtually untouched, five years later.

More importantly, taking proper care of ourselves is not to be reduced to practical hints and health tips. It starts with a much more basic challenge. Alongside the acquiring of skills and ministry strategies there is the complementary and demanding task of growing into a costly personal integration at all levels of our human identity and flourishing – emotional, theological, psychological, spiritual and social. We will not be effective ministers to others unless we have a mature and developing awareness of ourselves.

## Learning how to love

We need to agree on two things before we go any further. First, you cannot care for someone well if you do not really like them. Perhaps that sounds rather obvious. Behind this chapter lies the conviction that there is a right self-love that is essential to our sustaining and flourishing as human beings. Much painful evidence exists to show that this is something that those in ministry find hard to acknowledge and harder still to give themselves. It may be because this kind of love is assumed to be selfish. Aren't Christians called to deny themselves? Christian service is therefore about not paying attention to ourselves.

But the call to self-denial is actually damaging unless the following distinction is understood. Self-denial is not the same as self-rejection. It is closer to the joyful self-giving love expressed in Christian marriage. The sacrifice of Christian service is the response of humanity to the unconditional gift of divine love. We love because we have been loved first (1 John 4.19).

Self-denial that does not flow out of gratitude will actually be self-rejection. It may look very spiritual but it is deeply destructive of ourselves let alone of others. What does a minister gain if they fill the whole church and lose their soul?

Secondly, you can't look after someone effectively unless you take time to get to know them well. If this is true in relationships with others it is equally true of caring for ourselves. As with all significant relationships it takes commitment, time and energy. And like all relationships it will be as demanding and elusive as it is joyful. It requires that we give ourselves the same kind of listening and loving attention that we expect to give to others as ministers.

One of the things that makes this hard is the nature of Christian ministry. Our calling is to live for others. We spend a great deal of our time deeply immersed in the lives of others. This is demanding and can easily leave us with little time or energy left over for anyone else. It is perilously easy to lose touch with ourselves.

This discussion has already come a long way from exercise bikes and planning an evening out. Where do you begin to answer the question, 'how well do I look after myself?' What follows is neither prescriptive nor comprehensive. There is, of course, a contradiction in writing a 'self help' chapter that then tells you what you should be doing! As women and men in local church ministry we come to the issues of self-care and nurture with widely varying personalities and experience, at different stages of life and commitments, and ministering in contexts that make very different demands upon us. So I have focused on three areas of shared experience in ministry and use these as a way of illustrating what the responsibility to self-care might require in the midst of faithful ministry. Some questions are offered from time to time to encourage further reflection.

# Transitions

Life is an experience of continuous transition. At every level of our existence we experience ourselves as creatures in process. Christian discipleship is also an experience of journeying, growing and transformation. We are not yet human beings. We are human *becomers* – unfinished and even unclear what we may yet become. To be in ministry is to walk with people through the pain, confusions and possibilities of their life transitions. As with so many areas of our work we may not be as good at looking after ourselves in those times.

It may be that one important period of transition has led you to pick up this book. You may have recently moved to leadership in a new church – or you may be anticipating such a move. But even if you are now relatively established in your present context, the particularly vulnerable intensity that surrounds those early weeks and months in a new job is not quickly forgotten.

Something new can only begin if something else has come to an end. Endings are important. They are also difficult to negotiate and need care and time. For church ministers this is not easy. The parish profile prepared on a vicar's departure to attract a successor may be the nearest thing to a critique or review of their ministry in that place. But it was not written for them and they are supposed to have no part in it. In parish ministry contact with one's predecessor or the person coming after is traditionally discouraged. The break with the community that work and life have been shaped around (probably at some cost) can feel abrupt and very final.[1]

So how was it for you? It is worth adding that unless your new job 'found you' you may have been living with a degree of personal transition for some time before you were aware of it or felt able to act on it. The average length of time clergy spend looking for a move is presently two years.

---

**What were your thoughts and feelings on leaving your last post?**

**If you are married and have children or other dependent relatives what did leaving mean for them?**

**If you are single what did leaving mean for your primary relationships?**

---

How we begin is just as significant. Our beginnings bring a whole new set of changes and challenges on top of the adjustments we are still making to our endings. You may have arrived with a deep sense of call. But you will still be starting a new job, creating a new home, moving to a new region, entering a new culture, joining a new community, making new relationships, taking on new professional responsibilities. There is no short cut to this. It was said of Abraham that when he arrived where God was calling him he pitched his tent and 'lived as a stranger in the land of promise' (Hebrews 11.9). That expresses the task very well.

In the process of moving, the practical demands will be generally accepted and understood. But we will also be establishing a new relationship with *ourselves* (and with those who have moved with us). Out of our familiar patterns, routines and comfort zones we will be meeting ourselves in new contexts, facing new demands, responding to new challenges. It may have been some years since we last found ourselves so out of routine. How does it feel? We may be surprised to discover how vulnerable we can be or how quickly we get tired or overwhelmed. We may not recognize ourselves in our responses to these new demands.[2]

We are now much more aware of how significant the experiences of the first months and years of human life are for shaping our emotional needs and the kind of people we may become. That is not to suggest people cannot change but it does acknowledge that this period of life is especially formative and needs special care. There are many signs that the same is true of the early stages of our significant life changes. Pastoral evidence reveals that when facing a crisis or stresses later in ministry our response will be shaped, at least in part, by our earliest experiences of transition and change in ministry. The way we care for ourselves in the demands of transition establishes patterns that we continue to live by.

When you move, 'a thousand daily habits change'. Everything needs thinking about and remembering. There are no routines and memories of place for any of us to relax into. For three months after moving to my present home I kept going to the wrong drawer for my socks each morning. This actually unsettled me more than the new job itself!

In those early days you don't know whose voice is important and whose is misleading. You don't know what issues can be kicked into the long grass and which need to be top of the agenda. The task reminds me of my experience of being fitted with hearing aids. You don't just hear what you want to hear. Suddenly *everything* is loud! You have to learn to distinguish between noise and signal.

There is a natural concern to hit the ground running and make an impact but there is no short cut into the heart of a community as its new leader. We might spare ourselves more if we realize that the community too is facing major transition because we have arrived. This is not because we are already imposing our grand vision. We are just *different* – our presence, our manner, the way we speak, preach and lead worship. Arriving in one church I privately decided to not change anything for the first six months. And after six months I was accused of making too many changes!

So how long does it take to arrive? This varies for everyone. The combination of moving home, job and community scores high on life stress scales. This will also be true for those who have moved with us. Research shows that the process continues to impact significantly upon our energies and concerns for at least 18 months.

---

**What did arriving feel like?**

**Whoever else moved house for your job it is quite likely that you will be the first to find life settling into some kind of shape. What concessions do I need to make to enable their transition?**

**What is your most personal need at this point in your life?**

---

Some life transitions are more visible than others – such as leaving home, new job, marriage or parenthood. Others are more subtle. They may be influencing us for some time before we recognize that something is going on that we need to attend to. We need time and support as we enter into the 'yeses' that have brought us to this place. I was four years into ministry in one parish before I recognized that my 'yes' to being in that place was still hesitant. It had been a time of exciting growth but also some painful conflict. There were places within where my 'yes' to this call had yet to be made complete.

The same happened again in a later move to a very fulfilling ministry. I slowly became aware that I was restless and unsettled but had no idea why. My wife encouraged me to seek out someone to talk to. What emerged was not a problem to be solved, but a part of me that needed listening to because in the depths there were still important parts of myself that were adjusting to the radical changes recent years had brought.

What space do we allow for our journey through the stages and seasons of life? How do we respond, for example, to the questions and feelings that may be rising from our depths as we enter mid-life? When it is your job to represent the public faith of the church and to inspire its worship and prayer some transitions can be very unsettling. We may still feel required to be a leading a church with the stamina and certainties of someone who existed 20 years ago. 'More often than not the onset of mid-life is not dramatic. Denial is our first reaction to mid-life. Those who have long given themselves to others often have the greatest difficulty in taking their own needs seriously. Everything that was nailed down has come loose ... [there is] the loss of absolute certainty, the loss of a sense of one's invulnerability, and the loss of naiveté about one's single-mindedness. That God may be our immediate troubler as well as our ultimate peace is precisely the issue. It is no longer life's morning. It is at least the afternoon, and we move toward evening. Might mid-life just be God's traumatic gift to recall us to become ourselves?'[3]

---

**What season is your life in at the moment?**

**How are you experiencing living through it?**

---

We find ourselves in Christian leadership at a time when the Church in this country is facing critical challenges. Attendance and financial resources are in steady decline. The outcome is not certain. We are being asked to manage decline and plan for growth at the same time. Many denominations are launching strategies aimed at re-shaping patterns of ministry and developing 'new ways of being church'.

The radical change of a whole institution and its way of life – which is the task facing us – means we are asking for huge changes of self-perception and vocation as well as skills and methods among those who work within it.

One of the questions surfacing most frequently among clergy seeking counselling is the basic question of identity. 'Who am I?' 'I am not sure I recognize myself or my ministry in this struggling and demanding institution that keeps telling me I must radically change what I have been doing and still feel called to do.' It is no failure at such a time to feel you need to ask for help and support.

---

**How do you experience yourself in relation to the Church and what is being asked of you?**

---

## Identity

### Who do you say that I am?

One of the extraordinary privileges of Christian ministry is the range of people you meet in the course of work and the depth to which you can be welcomed into people's lives at all levels of human joy and pain. It is a holy trust and even when it is costly it can be immensely fulfilling. But one of the draining aspects of church ministry is the sheer confusion of roles and expectations that you can be asked to fulfil. Consider that in the course of one short Sunday morning you can be asked to relate to people as teacher, counsellor, worship leader, intercessor, administrator, friend, father or mother (regardless of your gender), husband, wife, confessor, healer or manager. In addition to that, a leader is asked to hold something of the story of the community – its hopes and fears. Much of this happens at an unconscious level but the burden is real. It was rather reassuring to hear of one very experienced therapist tell how taken aback he was when he was ordained as an Anglican priest. Despite all his professional experience of 'transference' and group dynamics he was quite unprepared for the sheer weight and power of projected hopes and expectations that he now experienced in his new role in the community.

To be the spiritual leader is to be a powerful symbolic figure in the community. You will also know very personal things about many of its members. In such a position you readily become the focus of divine hopes, idealized longings and unmet needs that actually belong elsewhere and are the responsibility of other relationships. This can be very seductive, particularly if other parts of life and ministry are less fulfilling. I can rather enjoy feeling needed and having this 'caring leader' role. Ministers need somewhere to reflect on what roles they are being asked to carry in the community. Some of these will be subtle and even unconscious to a degree. They will often feel flattering even if they are hard to bear.

Being a leader in an institution that is increasingly marginalized and insecure, the hunger for the affirmation of such a role is very real. Clergy need a strong sense of personal identity if they are not to get caught up in the confusion of this.

The issue of identity surfaces at the very beginning of St John's Gospel. It begins with John the Baptist in mid-argument with the Pharisees who are trying to find out who he is. But he will not introduce himself or his ministry. He does not allow himself to be known at all except in relation to Jesus. As the questions keep coming his answers get shorter and terser.

> 'Who are you?'
>
> 'I am not the Messiah.'
>
> 'Are you Elijah?'
>
> 'I am not.'
>
> 'Are you the prophet?'
>
> 'No!'
>
> (John 1.19-22)

For John the Baptist the secret of our identity in ministry begins with knowing who we are not! The relationship between our role and our identity outside our work is important in any walk of life. But when your job is to officially represent God, the need for clarity in this takes on a new urgency. Perhaps every minister should have this as a sign over their door and on their desk: 'I am not the Messiah!' And every minister's family should have a sign up saying 'And we are not the Holy Family either!'

Jesus himself insisted on the priority of knowing who he was called to be and refusing to accept any other roles. On one well-known occasion a man came up to him and said, 'Good Teacher, what must I do to inherit eternal life?' Whether spoken in flattery or out of respect you might have thought that Jesus of all people could have let it pass. But Jesus was very firm. He refused to be burdened by the task of fulfilling this man's expectations of him. He had to be free to be himself. In the process he was also willing to risk losing the man for the sake of the truthful speaking. 'Why do you call me good? No one is good but God alone' (Luke 18.18-19). Only then did he begin to respond to the man's question.

## The burden of being good

One of the hardest roles to negotiate in leadership is that of the idealized role model. It is encountered in many forms and different personalities will experience it in different ways. Perhaps the most common and burdensome of these is the requirement to be 'good' and 'loving'. There is nothing more tiring than having to be 'nice' to everyone – and Church leaders are required to be especially nice! They are not allowed to be angry or unreasonable. What vicar hasn't come across resentment at something a predecessor let slip 20 years ago (probably under extreme provocation), never to be forgotten or forgiven?

> **Unless we find a way of negotiating this pressure, ministry can lead to a narrowing of our emotional responses to life and relationships. A vicar whose only strategy is to smile at everyone while holding a lid on whatever emotions are actually fermenting beneath the surface will be in danger of emotional exhaustion. The burden of being good is a significant contributor to burn out in ministry. It is also true that our feelings do not decompose if we try to bury them. They will always be there or emerge in other less appropriate forms of expression. It is often those closest to us who carry the burden of what we are not facing about ourselves.**

One very practical reason why this pressure is hard to resist is that church ministers are leaders of voluntary organizations. If people decide they don't like what they see they will go somewhere else (and take their gifts and money with them). It is an unusually thick-skinned minister who does not feel the anxiety of this at some time or other. But while this anxiety controls relationships between a leader and the community no mature growth will be possible for either side. More crucially in the context of this chapter, the leader is being emotionally held to ransom by the community. The ministry now being offered is based on forms of emotional manipulation and seduction.

It took me a long time to realize that I did not have to pretend to agree with people if I didn't. I am still not good at it. It doesn't mean being rude or abrupt. It is actually giving the other person respect by entering the discussion with my own opinion. Those who want their vicar to confirm them in their prejudices usually change the subject at this point, but very often the conversation takes a dive deeper into something much more fulfilling. When I do this I establish an important personal boundary without which a real relationship is not possible.

What minister hasn't had the experience of feeling completely trapped in a pastoral relationship that leaves them exhausted, anxious and seriously tempted to murder! The reason will be as varied and complex as the people involved. But reflecting on my own experience I now consider the 'problem relationships' often began with poor management of the burden of being 'good'. I began by trying to be too 'nice'. It resulted in a failure to establish a personal boundary, based on truth. Sometimes it was my own anxiety to be liked and respected as a caring pastor. At other times it was a genuine concern to express care for people in their need. Either way what was offered as pastoral care was received by the other person as a collusive agreement with their prejudices and concerns.

> **Christian goodness is neither bland nor passive. The 'goodness' and 'love' modelled in the human life of Jesus includes the whole range of strong and sometimes volatile emotions. This is surely the secret of his vitality. The issues are often most sharply focused in situations of conflict and anger. Ministry needs the whole range of our passions to sustain and fulfil it.**

Here Christian idealism ('surely as Christians . . .') often colludes with a fear of conflict. This results in a repressing of the honest confrontation that is most needed. Anger is not wrong, of course, but it is a very powerful emotion within us and we may have good reason for fearing its destructive potential. The trouble is not that we get angry, it is that our anger does not end up doing what it is intended to do. Expressed positively we get angry because things matter, because we care deeply and we are personally involved. There is a vitality in anger isn't there? It is energizing. It is an energy we need. In fact if we try to live without these more turbulent passions we will be cutting ourselves off from some of our deepest sources of life and creativity. The alternative is no easier. Because they are so powerful it takes a great deal of energy to keep these passions underground. While living in fear of losing our tempers our actual need may be to find them in the first place. The root of some forms of depression lies here. Depression has been defined as 'anger without the enthusiasm'.

So what do ministers, robed in all the idealized expectations of Christian goodness and sanctity, do with the more shadowy side of themselves? I mean the bits that continue to resist conversion – the unreasonable bits, the untamed energies, the voices that mock all our attempts at holiness and remind us how far the public image is from the real thing. Only some of this needs confessing as sin. We need saving as much from our understanding of goodness. What may yet emerge is a more vital, more alive, more authentic disciple who is also a minister.

---

**What are the main roles you carry as a minister? How do you live with them?**

**What do you do when you just need to scream?**

**Where are the places you can take time off being 'good'?**

---

## Ambition and recognition

You are not supposed to 'do' ambition if you are a Christian, and especially not if you are a Christian minister. I don't agree. Of course there is a self-seeking, a desire for status or attention that is sinful and ultimately self-destructive. But Christian discipleship is not a passive conformity. God has made us people who desire things. We dream dreams. We make choices. We are alive in this. What I am talking about is a godly motivation to be someone who is growing, fulfilling our potential, serving God and others, making the best of the gifts and opportunities that are being given us.[4]

The reality is that, as an institution, the Church has a very flat career structure. There are relatively few senior posts to go on to. There is also less width in terms of choice and variety of ministry than there used to be. It is possible to feel trapped in a certain stage of ministry and to feel that there is no way out.

In other professions our training and experience would be recognized both in terms of promotion to greater responsibility and the reward of higher income. It can be very painful to see this happening for friends who entered their careers at the same time you entered ministry.

This means we must look for other ways of creatively developing our life and gifts in ministry. The advice of one bishop to his clergy feels wiser than ever. He always encouraged them to be developing a personal interest or specialism. This is not an area that immediately related to their present tasks, but would be part of their life-long learning and personal development. It is not just churches that need to be growing.

It is important to be honest about our longings and frustrations when we become aware of them. Christian ideals about humble service are particularly unforgiving forms of punishment at times like these. There is right need for recognition and expression of the worth of who we are and what we do. This is not to be spiritualized away. The issue here is not just about our future hopes. We will also need to be aware of how we feel about our past and how we feel about what we have achieved so far. Listening to that sense of missed opportunity or frustration at the way our life has unfolded may suggest the influence on us of the lives we have *not* had.[5]

The title of a major study of clergy stress and well-being sums up the need very clearly. Ministry needs both 'affirmation and accountability'.[6] The need for recognition is right and nurturing. Christian ministry is very hard to measure and is not offered within the clear time boundaries of, say, a day at the office. Pastoral care and spiritual support are also very intangible. It is possible to reach the end of a very long day having offered costly, skilled ministry in the place of human pain and confusion. But you may not have the satisfaction of anything being 'finished'. It may in fact be as unresolved as ever. There is no clear desk to enjoy. You may be carrying the burden of confidentiality. There is not even the public satisfaction of a job seen to be done well.

In such work it is easy to lose a sense of personal and professional worth.

---

**What do you want?**

**If you were to develop a personal interest further what might it be?**

---

# Embodiment

## Taking flesh

Etty Hillesum, the Dutch Jew who chronicled the Nazi occupation of the Netherlands and who died in the Holocaust, wrote, 'It is difficult to be on equally good terms with God and your body.' Is this your experience? For much of its history the Western Christian tradition has struggled to keep flesh and spirit apart. The flesh was treated as a temporal enemy and the home of all that is fallen and sinful. Spiritual and intellectual life was the ideal. Holiness required a renunciation of the flesh and its disordered desires. The word 'flesh' conjures up something elicit or forbidden rather than warm, living embodiment. This ambivalence is the more surprising in a faith that celebrates the doctrine of the incarnation at its heart. 'This is my body, given for you.' We meet God in our human flesh. Christian discipleship is about taking flesh, not renouncing it. For one theologian this remains a problem of such destructive consequence that he will not lead a Bible study without including a time of physical movement as part of it. There was wisdom too in the monastic pattern of combining prayer with manual labour.

Christian heirs of such an ambivalent tradition are probably going to need help to know what to do with their bodies. Clergy spend a great deal of time living in the mental, spiritual and affective dimensions of their personality. They can lose touch with their bodies and the vocation to embodiment. Ministry easily becomes subtly dehumanizing.

Our experience of life is inescapably physical. 'Movement is our first language. We move in the womb, and experience the movements and heartbeats of our mothers. Rhythm, well-being, joy, anxiety, distress are all communicated through these early movement experiences. Before language even starts to develop, our bodily interaction with our carers gives us the necessary scaffolding to develop person knowledge.'[7] This is underlined by the experience of people who have suffered particular abuse or personal degradation. Helen Bamber has spent her life working with victims of torture. She writes, 'cruelty is above all an experience of the body.' The work of rehabilitation and healing for such victims is to help them reclaim 'the good body' and this involves relearning a way of respecting the body and the self within it.[8] This requires more than keeping physically fit. There is a relationship to be nurtured. Our bodies absorb our stresses, pressures and anxieties. They may protest or let us down. The relationship may be painful. We may need to be reconciled to our bodies. They remind us of parts of ourselves and our approach to life that we are trying to ignore.

But our bodies can also make a positive contribution to the managing and healing of what burdens us. Physical exercise is known to be enormously therapeutic for the managing of stress.

The rule seems to be that if we treat our bodies as life companions they will be our allies in the search towards wholeness and integration. What is not an option is to live dis-embodied or simply treat our physical body as the equivalent of a hire car or supermarket trolley.

---

**Francis of Assisi called his body 'brother ass'.**

**What place has your 'body' and 'flesh' had in your human and Christian maturing?**

---

## Living passionately

The struggle to live in the sheer, raw physicality of our humanity is nowhere more evident than in relationship to our sexuality. This is a particularly vulnerable and complex area of our life to care for well. The high levels of anger and anxiety that dominate church debate on issues of sexuality simply add to the difficulty.

By sexuality I do not mean genital expression in the first instance. Sexuality, rooted in our bodily identity, is an expression of the whole of who we are in all our passions and desires. A conscious and healthy sexuality is therefore not necessarily genitally active. But we do need to be people who are in touch with the intensity and power of these passions within us. This primary drive within us leads us towards God and towards each other. It is that that makes it so desirable and fulfilling and leaves us so exposed and vulnerable before its power.

None of this is easy in a society unable to understand, for example, the difference between intimacy and genital sex. Nor is it easy in a Church struggling to find a way of talking about sex at all and that no longer has a positive understanding of the gift of celibacy and how to support it. Ministry today is offered in an age characterized by high levels of sexual confusion and wounding. Sexual and spiritual desire are closely related. This is not wrong but the two are easily confused. It requires discipline, personal honesty and a discerning awareness of our own ongoing needs to keep them in proper perspective.

We always bring in to pastoral encounters our own needs and hungers. We must learn to manage them appropriately. Ministry is often very lonely. This will be experienced in different ways but at some level it leaves us emotionally hungry. It is very costly to have to give yourself to someone else's personal pain when you are longing for that kind of loving attention for yourself.

Most denominations now publish guidelines for good pastoral conduct. These recognize that ministry is often given and received in private, one-to-one situations; highly personal confidences are shared; people are vulnerable and looking for loving support. The blurring of boundaries at such times is perilously easy. There is a need for clear professional discipline if trust is not to be abused. Practical advice includes keeping an open appointment diary. One of the first signs that an inappropriate relationship may be developing will be the temptation to add meetings and not openly record them. The immediacy and privacy that email enables also need considering. A level of informality is easily established in email communication that may not be helpful or appropriate.

In times of sexual temptation and tension in the course of ministry the first need is for honesty. St John calls this 'living in the light' (1 John 1.6). This may include some expression of sacramental confession. Confession is not only concerned with sin. Our unmet longing, pain and confusion will also find help and support here. It may be helpful to talk through what is going on with a counsellor or professional friend.[9] To bring it into the light in this way expresses a commitment to not hide or play games and opens the possibility of receiving helpful wisdom.

But when it comes to our own personal needs and hungers the issue will not be resolved by simply keeping the rules or avoiding awkward situations. We need some way of asking what is really going on. What is it that I actually want? Even at the height of sexual tension the answer may not be as obvious as it seems. Sexual release may be a way of avoiding our real hunger and desires, not of fulfilling them. We must learn to listen to our desires and wants. They are telling us things we need to hear.

---

What do I want?

What might 'growing' involve in this expression of my life and identity?

What are your particular needs for intimacy and where may you hope to find yourself supported and loved in them? This question is relevant to everyone but the responses will reflect very different contexts and needs – for example the varied lifestyles of single people in ministry.

---

# Boundaries and belonging

Our life as embodied, sexual beings constantly reminds us that we are created for relationships. Even the ache of loneliness may be a mercy if it reminds us of this. There is no such thing as a whole person in the sense of someone complete in themselves. We are made for each other. We know ourselves in community.

This is another important area for clergy self-care. Where the job is to be pastorally involved with people there can be a tendency for all relationships to feel like work. There will always be two factors involved here. I can feel frustrated when other people seem unable to treat us as ordinary human beings. But I may have difficulty in stepping out of role myself. How we handle this will vary from person to person but the issue for all of us is how we manage our personal and professional boundaries.

Boundaries enable two things to happen that are vital to our personhood and relating. They first of all allow a separation to happen. This is a positive separation. All relationships need a space between. Relationships that are only measured by how close we are to each other will quickly become suffocating. Secondly, boundaries provide a place of encounter. This is where we meet each other. Working out personal boundaries in ministry is not easy. Pastoral roles and relationships are complex and so are our responses to them.

## Closing the door

One important boundary is around the clergy home. Modern vicarages are designed with two front doors. The first leads into a small hall off which are found the vicar's study and toilet facilities for visitors. The second is an inner front door which separates home from work. It is a practical and caring provision but in practice it is much harder to keep the two separate. There is no mental door that shuts out a difficult pastoral crisis or unfinished preparation for Sunday. Furthermore, our home may be regularly used for church hospitality, ministry or home groups.

How welcome or invasive this feels will vary according to a variety of factors. If ministry is particularly demanding, the issue of personal space and the ability to detach from the job will be much more important. It will also be a factor for partner and family. During one particularly difficult period of ministry, as a single person, I had a need to get right out of the parish on my day off while simultaneously resenting the feeling of being 'driven out of my own home'.

Very few of those who represent the caring professions now actually live in the community in which they work. For clergy, living in an urban priority area or remote rural vicarage will not just have an impact on work, it will influence how they feel in their home. There will be issues of personal security as well as a need for space and refreshment.

Compared to previous generations of clergy there are many more practical resources for guarding the boundaries. A separate telephone line for personal and family use is an accepted way of keeping boundaries at important times. The increasing use of a parish office enables parish business to be helpfully screened. In some places the minister now works from the parish office. The home may not even be in the parish and is not publicly marked as the vicarage at all. The patterns of clergy home and work will become even more varied in the future.

## Looking the part

With church leadership comes a public profile in the community. How this is managed needs thinking through. One traditional clergy boundary was the uniform. In a more formal and hierarchical society the role and authority that went with it was recognized and respected. Today not only is that uniform not well understood, but our culture is marked by aggressive informality. Everyone is on first name terms. There is deep ambivalence towards uniforms and formal expressions of authority.

There will be very different views on this but the question in this context is – 'what are you wanting to say by what you wear?' This is an issue of both boundary and belonging. What we wear expresses our place in a community and how we wish to be known and recognized. All clothing (not just robing) is symbolic. So much is obvious. A huge fashion industry thrives on this fact. It is for this reason that I want to suggest that the issue of clergy 'uniform' is a more subtle one than is often acknowledged. Within the Church there is a common assumption that robing and clerical collars now create a separation. Well, actually, that is what uniforms are for. Each generation has to negotiate how it recognizes the boundaries of delegated authority and representative roles. For all its cheerful informality our age is characterized by the widespread breakdown of relationships due to the loss of secure social boundaries. For some at least the choice of certain clothes for work may help to establish a more careful boundary between public and personal, work and leisure, office and home.

## Living in time

Any job worth doing will be draining and have its times of stress. The problems come if these are prolonged and not balanced by times that resource and refresh us. It is also true that the demands of pastoral leadership are not evenly spread. So the principle of taking regular time off is vital but also needs to be applied with flexibility. The clergy 'day off' is meant to be that place. It belongs, of course, as part of a wider cycle of work, rest and holiday through the year. I want to suggest that the idea of the day off needs to be explored much more imaginatively. Different contexts of work may require different provision for rest and switching off. Personalities will also vary as to what works for them.

The majority of people in the community around us probably have two days off a week. If they work for the Church during their spare time, that is their choice. For them it is not the same as going into work on their day off. This is therefore not a reason for feeling guilty about minister's time off. There is a real difference between choosing to work in recreational time and doing six days a week in your full-time job. Some people argue that leading a full Sunday morning programme is, in terms of mental, emotional and spiritual demand, the equivalent of a full day's work.

Not everyone relaxes effectively in the inside of a day. I refer to it in that way because the 'day off' is more often the waking hours of the day. We will usually have worked the evening before. We then expect to be able to switch off and sleep well. Some people do this easily and re-energize quickly. Others will have barely begun to wind down by early evening of the day off and will then be feeling the pressure of the tasks they must resume in the morning.

The quality of my own time off in the parish was transformed when I began to stop work the evening before whenever possible. This is the Sabbath pattern. Some clergy take a day off and a 'Sabbath' day which they keep for personal study, reflection and prayer.

We need to take the principle of time off and in practice adapt it to our own needs. I know of a couple working in a very tough inner-city church who took extended time off each month and went away. This was the most effective way of caring for themselves and ensuring quality refreshment and time together in the demands of that particular ministry context.

Of course, there are times when we have to live with pressures in life and work that are not of our choosing. The space we really need is not possible. For example the needs of the children or the work patterns of our spouse can restrict what is possible. Conversely, a minister living alone may lack the routine distractions of company that helps to disengage and let go of work. At such times it is important to negotiate what is possible and receive it for the resource it is. The danger may come if this then becomes a pattern that is set and continues past the time when other provision may be possible. We need to build in times to review our managing of time, nurturing of relationships and quality of time off if we are not to settle for patterns of life that express subtle forms of self-neglect.

## I call you friends

There will be some clergy who are ministering in communities where there are high levels of shared interest and friendships form naturally and deeply. Others may be working in communities that are very different from those from which they have come. They feel like outsiders and life is lonely and isolating.

It is popularly believed that love is instinctive. But however much we wish it to be so, experience tells us that love is something we have to learn. We have to learn to give and receive love and that means learning to ask. It is possible for a minister to be struggling with personal isolation because they don't know how to receive friendship and love from their community. And there are congregations who leave their ministers feeling uncared for because they don't know how to offer it.

Teamwork and collaborative ministry are not new ideas in the Church, but the evidence is that working together does not come easily to clergy. If we are honest we are happier leading a team than being part of one. This kind of leadership is a form of self-defence and it is hard to break down. But learning to take the vulnerable risks of giving and receiving with supportive teams is more essential than ever.

For me one of the greatest gifts of friendship is that I can stop being responsible! We need help in taking time off being God. It is not good for us anyway. Sustaining and developing friendships outside of work need time, energy and planning. It means trying to ensure that we have time for people when we are not overtired ourselves. It also means planning time off when people other than fellow clergy are taking time off too.

But even with the best patterns of support there is no escaping the burden of isolation that comes with all leadership. In times when the winter of loneliness has set in on ministry life I have found wisdom in the story of the creation of Adam. In that perfect garden God is certain that one thing is not good – Adam is alone. This earth creature is made for relationship and needs to belong. Notice this is not a longing that God can fulfil. But the search for the particular communion he craves does not proceed as a hopeful series of blind dates, but begins with a journey into the whole of his world. 'Earth creature' must continue to be open to what is given – even if it is less than ideal. At times when the nurturing and warm companionship we crave is simply not there for us, the task is to be faithful to the ache and to go searching and reaching out to those who stand before us, naming and blessing them into our world.

Where can I be myself?

What might 'growing' mean for my relationships with people in the church?

Are there patterns of personal time and recreation that can be explored differently? If not, when will I next ask myself this question again?

## The importance of being unfinished

'If we are mad it's for God', says Paul with earthy and unexpected pragmatism (2 Corinthians 5.13). This statement is found in his most personal letter as he shares his experience of the sheer costliness of Christian service. The verse comes just before the passage often read at ordination services. It needs to be included. As we struggle to fulfil the seemingly irreconcilable range of expectations, demands and tasks that we call 'Christian ministry' we need that kind of rugged realism.

No one who has spent time with the themes in this chapter will easily confuse the task of looking after yourself with self-indulgence. It takes time and hard work. At times we may not know what is needed, what will help or what is possible. The task is never complete and no model is available of what a finished 'complete minister' product will look like if we manage to get it right. We will always be journeying, unfolding and unfinished.

Our search for good patterns of self-care, nurture and refreshment is responsible and life giving. But they can never be an end in themselves. Jesus constantly taught that to find the life we seek we must lose it (Luke 9.24). We must continually let go of our attempts to control and achieve our quest for wholeness for ourselves. Our story, with all its longings, will only be known as part of something much bigger and not yet revealed. 'We do not see what we shall become' (1 John 3.22).

What if we are in Christian ministry, doing what we are doing, not primarily because of our gifts and experiences (important though these are), nor by any earthly measure of usefulness or achievement (though in God's mercy we will be 'useful' more than we know)? We are where we are because God knows this is the shortest path to our final fulfilling in Christ. To be a Christian is to trust to Christ the mystery of who we are becoming. It is safe with him.

## For further reading

Chris Edmondson, *Minister – love thyself*, Grove Books, 2000.

Chris Edmondson, *Fit to lead – sustaining effective leadership in a changing world*, Darton, Longman & Todd, 2002.

Oswald Roy, *New Beginnings – a pastorate start-up work book*, Alban Institute, 2002.

Oswald Roy, *Clergy Self-care – finding a balance for effective ministry*, Alban Institute, 2001. See www.alban.org

Society of Mary and Martha, *Affirmation and Accountability – practical suggestions for preventing clergy stress and ill health retirement*, 2002; www.sheldon.uk.com

# 4

# Spiritual life

Felicity Lawson

Three years ago I moved back into parish ministry after posts in theological education and diocesan ministry. I quickly discovered why so many clergy are bad at replying to letters and returning forms: for the first time in 21 years I didn't have a secretary and if I didn't do something myself, it didn't get done! The relentlessness of parish ministry which I was experiencing was commented on not just by those who were incumbents for the first time but by experienced priests returning to parish ministry after a spell doing something else. Sundays came round quicker than I would ever have believed possible and there were never enough evenings in the week to fit in everything that needed to happen. Pastoral reorganization and the increase in dual role responsibilities only add to these pressures for many.

All of us who are incumbents have been ordained and come into parish ministry in response to what we believe to be a call from God. Our relationship with him is important to us. If it were not so we wouldn't be doing what we are doing. For many, the call to ordained ministry is costly. Like the first apostles who 'left their nets and followed Jesus', many have left behind successful careers, moved away from families and friends, endured misunderstanding. In my experience as a former Director of Ordinands, no one embarks on the course of exploring ordained ministry lightly: many, like Moses, Jeremiah and Jonah before them, try their best to argue with God and those who seem to sail through the selection processes often hit the wall later, during training or during their curacies. Vocation lies at the heart of Christian ministry yet for many clergy it can be the fulfilling of that vocation in terms of the outward expression of ministry that eats away at its core.

In his book *Called to Order* Francis Dewar[1] identifies three vocations which, he maintains, can often become confused. Our primary vocation is to know God, it is the call to basic Christian discipleship. Our second vocation is to become the person we have been created to be; celebrating, developing and using that combination of gifts and experience that is uniquely ours and growing into maturity of personhood in Christ. The third vocation is to particular, recognized and authorized ministries in the Church or the world: this includes, of course, the vocation to ordained ministry. The great danger for all who have experienced the third call is that it can begin to undermine the first two. And the relentlessness of parish ministry, the fact that there is always more to do and never enough time in which to do it, can be one of the biggest contributory factors.

Most of us have met the priest for whom the fire has gone out, the person who is simply going through the motions, or so it seems to us. What can happen for some people, and to a greater or lesser extent for others for whom everything on the surface still seems to be all right, is that they have hit spiritual or personal burnout.[2] They may have put so much into their vocation to ministry that they have neglected their primary and secondary vocations to know God and to become the person they were uniquely created to be. Sadly, as a result, the very ministry into which they have poured their whole selves suffers.

At our ordination the Bishop asks, 'Will you be diligent in prayer, in reading holy Scripture, and in all studies that will deepen your faith and fit you to uphold the truth of the Gospel against error?' This, like all the other questions, is designed 'that you may be strengthened in your resolve to fulfil your ministry'.[3] In writing this chapter, my thesis is very simple. If we don't take responsibility for ourselves before God, no one else will do so. Taking responsibility for ourselves involves recognizing that God loves us more than the ministries to which he has called us. Taking responsibility for ourselves involves investing time and energy into our primary and secondary vocations. If we do so, then far from suffering because of the time we have 'stolen' from it, our vocation to ordained ministry will be enhanced and enriched out of all proportion and will 'bear fruit to the glory of God'. Of course I am not saying that giving 'quality time' to our relationship with God is necessarily easy, nor am I claiming to be particularly good at it, but I am saying that I believe it is vitally important.

## Taking responsibility for ourselves

What then does it mean to take responsibility for ourselves under God? How can we guard and develop our relationship with God and that sense of value and self-worth which springs from knowing we are loved and cherished for ourselves and which, in turn, paradoxically frees us to give ourselves in sacrificial service to others? What follows are some of the areas that I have found important in my own life and which I find occur most frequently in spiritual direction with clergy. Set out like this, the list can look daunting: please remember it is offered as a resource not a requirement, a menu from which to choose rather than a spiritual feast one is obliged to consume.

## Know what nurtures you

We are all delightfully different. Some of us are extroverts: we gain our energy from engaging with other people. Others are introverts: we may be very good at relating to people but such social and pastoral interaction drains us. Some of us gain insights from books, others from sharing in groups, others from reflecting on experience. Spiritually some of us are uplifted by a large gathering, be it a charismatic celebration or a concelebrated Mass, while others long for space and silence. For some people, the physical environment in which we relate to God is important, while others hardly notice their surroundings.

One of the many insights gained from the Myers-Briggs Type Indicator (MBTI®) is that what works spiritually for one person will not necessarily work for another. Chester Michael and Marie Norrisey, in their book *Prayer and Temperament*, say: 'All indicators point to a close relationship between our innate temperament and the type of prayer best suited to our needs.'[4] They suggest that different spiritual traditions, specifically Ignatian, Augustinian, Franciscan and Thomistic, relate specifically to particular temperament types while others such as Benedictine or Teresian seem to be accessible to everyone. They go on to suggest that we should for the most part use the forms of prayer most suited to our temperament in our daily prayer because if we do, prayer will come more naturally and be less of a burden. However, some of our most powerful encounters with God may well occur when praying in ways with which we are less comfortable. In terms of MBTI this is because when praying in this way we are using what is known as the Inferior Function or praying from our Shadow and therefore less in control. The lesson seems to be that it is important to take time to experiment with unfamiliar forms of prayer, perhaps in our more leisurely moments such as a quiet day or retreat, but that the bread and butter of daily prayer should be in a form that suits our temperament.

However, one does not have to be an expert in MBTI in order to know oneself. If you have not done so recently, it may be important to take time to ask yourself: What helps me to engage with God – liturgical prayer, silent meditation, icons, creativity, Bible study, nature, music? Do I most naturally find God in the market place or the desert? Am I a lark or an owl? When am I at my best and do I give God prime time or only the times when I haven't the energy to do anything else? These are important questions to address if we are to take responsibility under God for our own spiritual well-being.

## Don't have too narrow a definition of spirituality

The Creator God enjoys his creation. The Incarnate God is present in the midst of the ordinary and the everyday. Many clergy get their fill of religion. Looking after ourselves spiritually doesn't necessarily mean adding to the religious aspects of our lives. Ignatian spirituality, which seems to be very popular at the moment, teaches people to 'look for God in all things'. A friend of mine, who is a sister in the order of the Institute of the Blessed Virgin Mary and who runs a retreat house, regularly goes and buys herself a good cup of coffee and people watches. It gets her away from the telephone and the demands of other people, it makes her sit down and do something she enjoys (a little treat reminds us we are all special to God and worth pampering occasionally), and in doing so it puts her back in touch with God and invariably gives God an opportunity to speak to her and for her to receive insights which she may not have heard in the busyness and demands of the centre. Another friend with a very demanding ministry swims at least once a week, thereby taking exercise in an otherwise sedentary job but also creating space and doing something she really enjoys. Someone else, who kindly read a draft of this chapter, has taken up the piano. When I have been engaged in a particularly demanding piece of ministry I will often go into the garden, if only for a few minutes, and pull up some weeds or deadhead some flowers – being close to nature has a regenerative effect. The planned and creative use of time off is important but what I am thinking about here is rather the deliberate taking of opportunities to reconnect with ourselves and God in the midst of daily ministry without feeling guilty about it. This is not of course a substitute for the routines of prayer, study and meditation which nurture our spiritual lives but an important adjunct to them.

## Building a pattern that works for you

Anglican clergy are bidden by the Canons of the Church of England to say the offices of morning and evening prayer daily. It is a primary part of our vocation as deacons and priests to pray for and on behalf of others: the fact that the offices provide a framework which also sustains our personal prayer is for many an added bonus. Some people, as we have already noted, thrive on routine, others need variety. Saying the daily office becomes the bedrock for many people's ministries, especially in times of difficulty or spiritual dryness. For others, attempting to say the offices daily may lead to guilt (because they never seem to 'do it properly') or frustration (because it is as 'dry as sawdust'). Many clergy find that they enjoy saying the daily office with others but really struggle to say it by themselves, although of course when we pray we are never praying alone because we join the great company of prayer being offered constantly around the world. In theological training and during the curacy this corporate aspect is often a given and one of the adjustments on entering a first incumbency is establishing and maintaining a pattern of daily prayer.

Bearing in mind the insights of Myers-Briggs, perhaps those who struggle with a routine of daily prayer need to look at the different elements within the office of praise, confession, intercession and Scripture and ensure that these are equally woven into the day but in a way which suits their temperament and not necessarily in a pattern which was originally designed for members of religious orders. The danger, of course, is that if we don't have the basic discipline of the offices, prayer or scripture, or both, can slip away unnoticed until it is too late.

It seems to me that many of the books on the spiritual life are written by people who enjoy routine: those who don't are often made to feel a failure before they have even begun! Developing a basic rule of life and sticking to it is easier for those who enjoy routine than for those who don't but a good spiritual director or companion will help us to build a discipline that is life-giving and suited both to our personalities and our needs at any particular time. In his Grove booklet *Finding a Personal Rule of Life* Harold Miller examines the pros and cons of designing our own rule or adopting a rule belonging to a particular religious society.[5] Most religious orders have tertiaries or companions who adopt a specially designed rule relating to but different from the rule followed by members of the order. Many clergy, who have never felt an affinity with the traditional religious orders, are finding great support and encouragement from belonging to one of the more contemporary communities such as the Community of Aidan and Hilda or the Order of Mission based at St Thomas Crookes in Sheffield, both of which have a clear vocation to mission and evangelism in contemporary society.

A healthy pattern, or rule of life, will have different elements some of which are daily, some weekly, some monthly and some annually. All will want to develop a pattern of daily prayer and Scripture including intercession for the Church and the world as well as for local needs. Some build into this a discipline of spiritual reading, perhaps using one of the books of short readings designed for the purpose,[6] or setting aside some time to read a few pages or a chapter of a particular book while others find reading just a few pages immensely frustrating and are better setting aside a longer time once a week. 'Silence is a constant source of restoration. Yet its healing power does not come cheaply. It depends on our willingness to face all that is within us – light and dark – and to heed all the inner voices that make themselves heard in silence.'[7] In silence we become aware of the many concerns which press in upon us but it is also in silence that we open ourselves afresh to hear God. The more contemplative among the clergy will include a period of silence in their daily prayer, others will do this less frequently, but for all of us it is an important discipline of the spiritual life not to be avoided simply because we find it difficult. The weekly routine should also include something which specifically nurtures us as a person, something we enjoy: sitting listening to some music, going for a walk, time in the gym, doing something creative, anything that reminds us that God delights in us and cares about us and not just the ministries he has called us to.

The sort of things which we may want to build in on an occasional basis are quiet days, retreats,[8] conferences, cell group meetings, visits to a spiritual director or soul friend and, of course, days off and holidays. These last points are about caring for ourselves, and our families and friends, and are an equally important part of staying healthy spiritually. The very best practice says that when we get a new diary the first entries should be days off and holidays, then retreats, quiet days and study days. If they are in the diary then we can always negotiate, but if they aren't, then it is all too easy to find that they get squeezed out by other pressing and important demands.

As well as specific times of prayer, we are bidden to 'pray constantly'. We pray as part of our pastoral ministry, both openly with people and also unseen as we hold them in the presence of God. We learn to 'play our holy hunches', to step out in faith obedient to the inner voice, to risk being a fool for God. Years ago I disciplined myself consciously to pray in tongues whenever I walked around the parish or drove on the motorway; now I find myself praying in this way without thinking about it. Not everyone, of course, prays in tongues: other people might use the Jesus prayer or some other spiritual discipline in a similar way in order to weave prayer into the routines of daily life.

---

Sometimes your prayer will be an experience of the infinite distance that separates you from God;

sometimes your being and his fullness will flow into each other.

sometimes you will be able to pray only with your body and hands and eyes;

sometimes your prayer will move beyond words and images;

sometimes you will be able to leave everything behind you and concentrate on God and his Word.

Sometimes you will be able to do nothing else but take your whole life and everything in you and bring them before God . . .

Remember prayer is more powerful than anything you can achieve by your actions.[9]

---

## Finding fellowship and support

In theory deanery chapter meetings should be a source of mutual support
and encouragement: offering an opportunity for clergy to pray together, study
together and share honestly with one another. Sadly this is not always the case
though I have belonged to some excellent chapters and I have seen others
transformed by a few people who are prepared to take the risk of being
genuinely open about both the joys and the pains of ministry. Another potential
source of fellowship and support is in an ecumenical group of local ministers,
especially when members are committed to action together as well as to praying
for one another. However, there are times when what is already in place does not
provide what we are looking for and then we have to take the initiative. About
once every six to eight weeks I meet for lunch with a former colleague: we
exchange news, chew the cud, have a good moan and generally put the world
to rights, we pray with and for one another and these regular but infrequent
meetings are supplemented by occasional emails or telephone calls. I often find
friendship and support from those involved in different Christian organizations in
which I serve as a trustee or committee member while a former colleague says
that he has often found the greatest support in the wider community, among
people who do not necessarily share his faith but with whom he has common
cause in the parish or locality. Others I know belong to organizations like the
Diocesan Evangelical Fellowship, New Wine Network or Society of Catholic
Priests and find encouragement and support from meeting with people with
similar convictions. The networks that clergy belong to will vary but the principle
of taking time for friendship, fellowship and support is important.

## The value of accountability

One of the problems for many incumbents is working alone. No one really sees
what we are doing, whether we are being good stewards of our time and talents,
whether we are being over-indulgent and only doing those things we enjoy, or
whether we are spending far too long in aspects of ministry for which we are
ill-equipped. For many who have entered ordained ministry later in life after a
career in teaching or business, this lack of accountability seems very strange.
Many dioceses are trying to address this with some form of ministry review but
the reality is that under most schemes the minister meets with a consultant once
a year if that, and the consultant may or may not be of the minister's choosing.
The scheme may or may not be flexible enough to meet the specific needs of
the individual and the constraints of the system and human frailty conspire to
mean that it is all too easy to play the system and avoid genuine accountability.
Once again it is important to take responsibility for ourselves.

Many clergy value the ministry of a soul friend or spiritual director,[10] someone with whom they meet several times a year, someone with whom they aim to be completely open before God. Despite an increasing number of training courses in spiritual direction, a good director is not always easy to find and persistence is often required. Most dioceses publish a list of spiritual directors or have someone who can act as a reference point. It is worth consulting them but it is also worth asking around as many of the best spiritual directors never make it to any list because they have always got more people wanting to meet with them than they have time available. A good director will always suggest a trial period, usually a year, and will take time exploring what the person seeking direction really wants or needs. For some clergy sacramental confession forms an important aspect of spiritual direction, others have a separate confessor, while for others the discipline is one they use only occasionally, if at all. At its best, sacramental confession helps a person to be honest with themselves as well as with God and enables them to know afresh the grace of forgiveness and acceptance that many clergy are very good at ministering to others but less good at applying to themselves.

Not everyone finds one-to-one spiritual direction helpful: for some people cell groups, which are often set up as people leave training, act as a form of corporate direction. Good cells will often work within an agreed framework giving a specific amount of time to each member for them to present some aspect of their life and ministry, the other members listening prayerfully and offering reflections in a disciplined manner. Other people find a form of accountability in a supervision group, often using a professional from another sphere such as counselling or social work as a facilitator.

## Journaling as an aid to reflection

One of the difficulties for those who live extremely busy lives and who work alone much of the time is remembering clearly what has happened; another is stopping to reflect on and learn from experience. The discipline of keeping a spiritual journal can help address this. In a profession where confidentiality is important and there isn't necessarily anyone around to talk things over with, it can also be very cathartic. Some people journal on a daily basis, others once a week, others more infrequently. The style is not important: the journal is for the benefit of the writer, no one else. Some use it to record information. Some see it more as a form of self-expression, perhaps writing poetry, sketching, inserting prayer cards or quotations. Others use it as a form of prayer.

Whatever the style adopted, and this will depend on the personality of the writer, the recording of the journal is only part of its value: the other part comes from periodically reviewing what has been written. Some people do this on their annual retreat or before going to see their spiritual director. Reviewing a journal allows one to see patterns and trends which can often be hidden in the demands of daily life – seeing the proverbial wood for the trees. Perhaps a verse of Scripture has been noted several times over a 12-month period. Perhaps a resolution to take action has been made but not implemented. Perhaps a relationship is demanding more time and energy than was realized. Things often become clearer with the benefit of hindsight.

Some people use a journal in connection with the Examen – a way of reflecting on life which originated within Ignatian spirituality. Put simply the idea is to look back at the end of a day or a week with a view to discerning where God has been at work. There is a twofold aim: (a) to discover and celebrate the love and grace of God in all things; (b) to be honest about where we have fallen short of God's will and purpose for our lives so that we can confess and receive forgiveness.

## Getting input and fresh ideas

Those who give out to others have a responsibility to ensure that they continue to be fed intellectually and spiritually. Our preferred learning styles will depend on our personalities: some learn best from books whereas others gain most from learning alongside others in study groups or conferences. Most people benefit from a varied diet and a degree of planning is important. Some things worth thinking about include:

- Maintaining a balanced programme of reading in spirituality, pastoral theology, biblical studies and doctrine as well as books and articles about contemporary society;

- Joining a clergy reading/study group or setting one up;

- Subscribing to a theological journal;

- Planning regular study days/reading weeks away from the parish;

- Attending conferences and training events;

- Making use of diocesan Continuing Ministerial Education training days and grants;

- Making an annual individually guided, preached or themed retreat;

- Requesting the PCC to pay for one conference or retreat per year;

- Belonging to or supporting a missionary society or parachurch organization.

# Making the most of parish life

One of the great dangers for anyone involved in public ministry is that our relationship with God becomes purely functional. There are, I believe, two different dangers.

When we are first ordained, or when we move posts, everything can seem terrifyingly new and demanding. We know we cannot fulfil even the simplest of tasks in our own strength: we pray about everything! After a while taking a funeral, planning the Sunday worship, writing the vicar's letter in the parish magazine becomes less personally and spiritually demanding. Our experience, skills and confidence increase and, although we wouldn't like to admit it publicly, we could undertake many of the routines of parish life without much reference to God. I remember being amazed at how the first incumbent with whom I worked could open the Scriptures at a midweek service and speak without a note and on Sundays he would go into the pulpit with just a scrappy piece of paper with a few jottings on it. Now I do it myself! Of course it is not that he, or I, speak without preparation or reference to God but over time we have learnt the skills of sermon construction and the thoughts shared are, hopefully, the fruit of lives spent in companionship with God and reflection on his word even when specific time for preparation has been limited through circumstances beyond our control. However, if I am honest, I am also aware that I do not always prepare as thoroughly for Sunday worship and other parish events as I once used to and that, like the Israelites once they had reached the promised land, there is a danger of settling down and taking God for granted. This neglect of actively seeking God in the routines of parish ministry can lead to a lowering of expectation that he will be at work in us and through us.

The other danger is that we only relate to God in terms of our ministry. So we only read the Scriptures with a view to the latest sermon or Bible study, we only pray for others and never for ourselves. But this is to forget that our primary vocation is to know God and be known by him, not as a minister of the gospel but as a unique human being in whom he takes delight. That is why it is important to take responsibility under God for maintaining our own spiritual journeys as well as exercising the ministries to which we have been called.

We must also remember that clergy have a primary responsibility for nurturing the spiritual life of others and there are ways in which we can work with the flow of parish ministry so that the life of the local church becomes a resource for ourselves as well as for other people. Here, once again, knowing ourselves and taking time to get to know the parish will be important if we are to exercise a wise and edifying ministry and not an abusive one.

Every parish has an image – the way it thinks about itself, and a reputation – the way in which others think about it. The two may coincide but they may not. For instance a parish may have a reputation for being charismatic when in fact it is only a small group within it who have been touched by the renewing work of the Holy Spirit. Or it may have a reputation for being Catholic because of the style of dress and form of liturgy preferred by the previous incumbent while the majority of the parishioners have no appreciation of the fundamentals of a truly Catholic spirituality. A new incumbent going to such a parish and believing only the reputation, without taking time to listen both to the spiritual history of the church and to individual members, is likely to make some very false assumptions. Acting on these can lead to unnecessary hurt and misunderstanding and so delay the further growth towards maturity in Christ of individuals and of the church. Like people, when one gets to know them, parishes are rarely as simple as they may at first appear. Just as a good spiritual director will spend time getting to know a new directee, asking questions and listening prayerfully to their story, so a new incumbent needs to listen to the Christian community of which they have become a part and so discern what needs to be affirmed and built upon from the past and where something new may helpfully be introduced.

To impose one's spiritual preferences on a parish without discerning their needs is nothing less than spiritual abuse. Nonetheless, as incumbents we may assume that one of the reasons we have been called to this particular place at this particular time is because we have something to share with them out of our experience of God's grace as well as something more to discover with them as we share this part of our spiritual journeys together. At its best, travelling together with a Christian community of which we have been called to be the leader can be a thrilling, if at times scary, adventure. God has always got more to teach us if only we are open to him and often he uses the most unlikely people as his tutors in the school of faith. Kingdom ministry has a mutuality about it which should enable us at times to be way out of our depth and learning from those around us and at others to be that tower of strength and stability which gives other people the security and freedom they need in order to learn and grow.

Because parishes are so different, it is dangerous to offer blueprints. What follows is simply a suggestion of areas of parish ministry which may be developed to the mutual enrichment of both incumbent and people.

## Encouraging prayer in the parish

One of the things many first incumbents miss is the routine of daily prayer with their training incumbent and others which should have characterized the curacy. In some parishes there is a tradition of parishioners joining the incumbent for morning or evening prayer. In others this would be a new concept. However, sensitively done, encouraging parishioners to join their incumbent for prayer can be both a support for the incumbent and an enrichment for those who come. The style of prayer will depend to a large extent on the tradition of the parish but the *Common Worship* versions of Morning and Evening Prayer encourage flexibility within a framework that should be adaptable to most contexts. The popular Franciscan *Celebrating Common Prayer* has a simplified version suitable for parish use and there are several different Celtic office books readily available as well as those linked with communities like Iona or Taizé. Care needs to be given to the timing of daily prayer if lay people are to join in: the traditional time of 8.00 a.m. is, in practice, too late for those going to work and too early for those who are retired or taking children to school. It may be that over the course of a week, provision needs to be made for both groups.

In addition to patterns of daily prayer, which will inevitably not be at a time to suit everyone, there should be opportunities other than Sunday and mid-week services where people can grow in prayer. The style of these gatherings for prayer will vary depending upon the tradition of the parish from the traditional evangelical or charismatic prayer meeting to a silent Julian group. Whatever the tradition, remember that there will be some people whose preferred way of praying does not fit with the parish norm or the personal preferences of the incumbent. It is important to provide a variety of approaches if all are to grow in the life of prayer. Such prayer gatherings may happen weekly, others monthly or even annually.

Although initially the incumbent may have to be involved in organizing and leading prayer events, the aim should be to train others to do so. When I moved to my present parish I instigated a week of prayer early in January: as well as the usual mid-week services, there is a time of prayer every evening ranging from guided meditation or prayer stations to a prayer and praise evening led by our worship group and a prayer walk around the parish on the Saturday morning. There is a different focus every year and resources for intercession are produced so that those who cannot easily come to the mid-week gatherings can nevertheless join in at home. During this week and several other times in the course of a year we will have a Day of Prayer, when the church is open and individuals are encouraged to sign up and come and pray for 30 minutes as well as joining in some corporate times of prayer dotted throughout the day. Other churches have nights or half-nights of prayer. The 24/7 Prayer[11] movement which began among young Christians is having a significant impact on many churches. Quiet days, either in the parish or at a local church or retreat centre, are also an excellent way of encouraging spiritual growth in members of the congregation. Inviting someone else to lead means that we are able to join in as a participant and share an experience of seeking God alongside our parishioners.

## Preparing for and leading worship

One of the many things for which I remain grateful to my first incumbent is the example he set and the expectation he had that all his staff would arrive 30 minutes before any service and spend time in prayerful preparation as well as the last minute practicalities of ensuring that books are in place and people organized. As a visiting preacher I have been amazed at how few other clergy follow this practice, but for me that time of quiet recollection and focusing afresh on God is essential if I am to be used to lead other people into his presence in a manner worthy of the one whom we are coming to worship. Over nearly 30 years this simple discipline has been a lifeline for me personally in the midst of a busy ministry.

If such preparation for worship is part of our lifestyle, then we can begin to encourage others such as Readers and musicians to make a priority of taking time to prepare: when those responsible for leading worship are seen to take this seriously, others will begin to be affected and the whole quality of our worship will be enhanced. As this is the main contact point for the majority of church members, thought, prayer and time spent in preparation both in advance of and immediately before worship will have a significant impact on the spirituality of the whole parish.

When it comes to longer-term planning for worship, one of the challenges of parish ministry is that the incumbent can never simply enter into the particular season being celebrated because of having to think ahead to what comes next. So as Lent begins we are already beginning to plan for Holy Week and Easter and no sooner have we begun to rejoice in the Resurrection than we are beginning to think about Pentecost. No wonder many clergy breathe a sigh of relief when we enter into the seemingly endless Sundays after Trinity. For those who, as lay people, have enjoyed and been nurtured by the pattern and variety of tone provided by the Church's year this always having to think ahead can lead to a quasi-schizophrenic feeling as well as adding to the sense of relentlessness which was mentioned at the beginning of this chapter.

One of the big adjustments most people have to make when they are ordained relates to the difference between sitting in the pew and being on the receiving end of someone else leading worship – albeit with the occasional foray to the front to read a lesson or lead the intercessions – and the responsibility for leading others. When we are being led in worship we are free to 'go with God', to let our minds wander and dwell on the verse of a hymn or a passage of Scripture, to make connections with our daily lives, even to be distracted and find ourselves thinking about something else entirely: we are carried by the flow and are able to slot back in to the mainstream after a brief excursion into what for most people might be an insignificant diversion but for us might have been a significant encounter with God. When we are leading worship we are always looking in several directions at once: part of our attention will be on the overall flow and direction of the service, on helping the congregation as a whole to engage with God, but we will also be wondering whether June will remember she is reading the lesson, whether Steve will ever stop rambling on in the intercessions or whether anyone will ever notice that the new couple sitting at the side are totally confused about which hymn book we are singing from now.

On Pentecost Sunday a couple of years ago we had prayer stations during the intercessions based on some of the symbols of the Holy Spirit: there was water for cleansing and refreshing, candles symbolizing the spreading of the gospel into dark places and anointing with oil for healing and commissioning for service. The worship group were leading us in song as people made their way to the different stations in response to the sermon. In order to speed things up slightly I had said that the anointing, like the other stations, would take place in silence which was just as well as I stood at the front anointing people while watching an elderly member of the congregation towards the back of the church collapse, be cared for by several nurses in the congregation and eventually leave in an ambulance – but not before I had made my way through the congregation to anoint him before he left. Thinking that everybody would be worried, I announced before the Peace that he was all right and that someone had gone with him and his wife to the hospital just to make sure there was nothing serious. Most people had been totally unaware of what was going on and were amazed when I told them: they had been going with the flow, I had been exercising the ministry of oversight. Everyone else came out of church commenting on what a marvellous service, I came out utterly exhausted!

Mercifully, not every Sunday is like that, but those at the front will always be aware of what is going on in a way that will not affect the majority of people in the congregation and although others may be helping to lead the worship, ultimately it is the incumbent who carries the responsibility even, in my experience, in services when they are not officially leading. Although it becomes easier with time, I don't think that we can ever hope to return to the place of simple participation in worship we once knew. Even on holiday I find myself thinking that something is a good idea or that I certainly wouldn't have preached on that passage in that way. The time when this is less true for me is when I am on a conference or a retreat where I both trust those in leadership and am consciously looking to receive from God for myself. Perhaps it is not surprising that a neighbouring parish where a member of the Liturgical Commission is incumbent and runs occasional evening services billed as 'charismatic worship within a liturgical framework' attracts a disproportionate number of clergy: we know that the services will be imaginative and well led and that we will be free to participate as members of the household of faith, receiving prayer ministry which is appropriate and confidential if we wish to avail ourselves of the opportunity.

### Planning for nurture and growth in discipleship

One of the most rewarding aspects of parish ministry is seeing people come to faith and grow in faith. The wonder of someone for whom God has become real and personal is infectious and can refresh the most weary or disillusioned minister. Of course that is not a reason for planning opportunities for people to explore and discover faith, but it is one of the positive spin-offs. Nurture groups are the single most effective means of bringing people to faith today yet only one in three parishes runs them as a regular part of their programme (see below pages 75–7). I have always found the research and preparation for these courses both stimulating and challenging to my own faith as I have had to think deeply about particular topics or issues in order to be able to enable others to think them through as well.

As well as running nurture and discipleship groups within the parish, both clergy and lay people will benefit from participating in events organized by others, be they another church, the diocese or one of the many para-church organizations. Such events offer inspiration, ideas and encouragement. Going away together, either on a parish weekend or retreat or joining in a national event like Spring Harvest, New Wine or the National Pilgrimage to Walsingham can strengthen the faith of individuals and deepen the bonds of fellowship within the group. As individuals only have a limited amount of time and finance to invest in such events it is worth thinking strategically about what one wishes to encourage, perhaps building a pattern over several years beginning with days and working towards residential events if these are a new idea for the congregation: simply recommending everything that arrives in the clergy mailing can lead to a dissipation of effort and effect.

## Riding out the storms

As the disciples discovered on Lake Galilee, storms can arise from nowhere without warning. In our lives these may be caused by serious illness or bereavement, a family crisis or problems in the parish: sometimes we see them coming and have time to prepare but it is often those that arrive unexpectedly, like the Galilean ones, which have the power to throw us off course. How people respond to crises depends on a number of factors such as personality, previous life experience and pre-existing levels of stress and exhaustion: something which may be handled in a relaxed manner on one occasion can, on another, be the proverbial last straw. Just as individuals have different thresholds for coping with physical pain, so too our capacities to cope with things like conflict vary enormously. Although I have learnt to face conflict and confront it when appropriate, it never ceases to amaze me that some people actually seem to enjoy and get a buzz out of it, even stirring things up if life becomes too boring and routine.

Problems at home, especially marriage difficulties or struggles with the children, pose a particular problem for the incumbent. Life at the vicarage often feels as if it is lived out in the full gaze of public view and there are times when this is particularly unhelpful. When disaster hits a member of the church family or the wider community, incumbents find themselves dealing not only with their own pain but also with everyone else's as well. As the priest and leader within the community, others look to them for strength, support and often for an explanation of the inexplicable, and they can find themselves in the full glare of the media, a role for which many feel very under-prepared. A more familiar scenario may be the serious illness of a child or young adult within the congregation: lay leaders may have totally opposing views of how to respond and the incumbent may become caught in the middle, for instance, between those who are praying for a miracle and accusing others of not having enough faith and those who are not at all convinced that this is how the church should be praying on this occasion.

How we cope with our own confusion and pain when tragedy strikes will be a key factor in our ability to help other people face theirs. When I was on the staff at St John's Nottingham, one of our very able and attractive young students was killed in a tragic climbing accident just after the end of the autumn term. The principal was responsible for organizing a memorial service but as chaplain I was responsible for leading the opening service of the new term. Before I could begin to prepare, let alone lead, that service I had to seek out my spiritual director and ask him to help me scream at God. Not for the first time in my ministry I was grateful that I had some of the support structures mentioned earlier in this chapter already in place.

Sometimes the storms that arise appear to be simply the 'slings and arrows of outrageous fortune', the painful reality of living in a fallen and broken world, but at other times it is as if they are being co-ordinated by a malevolent force set to undermine what God is doing. Over 30 years of Christian ministry I have become convinced of the reality of spiritual conflict, of what Paul calls the principalities and powers opposed to God. As C. S. Lewis wrote in his preface to The Screwtape Letters: 'There are two equal and opposite errors into which our race can fall about the devils. One is to disbelieve in their existence. The other is to believe, and to feel an excessive and unhealthy interest in them. They themselves are equally pleased with both errors and hail the materialist and the magician with the same delight.'[12] Whether or not one wants to use Lewis's terminology, a wise incumbent will remain alert to the possibility of a supernatural dimension in conflicts and crises and seek to discern and pray accordingly. Whether confronting overt evil, or as is more often the case, facing a mixture of human frailty and spiritual forces of darkness, I have always found the prayerful support and wise counsel of members of religious communities to be of enormous benefit.

## Deeper into God

In drawing this chapter to a close, I want to return full circle to Francis Dewar's different types of vocation, for it has been my experience that far from being in conflict with one another, rightly pursued our different vocations can greatly enrich and enhance one another. A life lived in openness to God and to other people will draw us ever more deeply into that mystery which is the Holy Trinity; it will lead us both into the vulnerability and the joy of God. In seeking to lead others into a deeper knowledge of God, I myself am challenged to ask questions about the kind of God I believe in; in seeing his unconditional love and grace at work in others, I am exposed afresh to the gospel; in holding others before him in prayer, I too discover more of its costly stripping and transforming power. We, like those we are called to lead, are on a spiritual journey: to be called to minister to God's people is not only at times immensely costly, a sharing in Christ's sufferings, it is also an enormous privilege and great joy, a sharing in the power of his resurrection. In the words of Paul to the Christians at Philippi, 'Not that I have already obtained this or have already reached the goal; but I press on to make it my own, because Christ Jesus has made me his own' (Philippians 3.12).

# 5

# Direction: discerning and communicating vision

## Chris Edmondson

> You see things as they are and ask 'Why?' But I dream of things that
> never were and ask 'Why not?'

> George Bernard Shaw

Whatever else might be involved, fundamentally I believe that leadership is
concerned with vision, seeking a vision for the particular context into which the
leader is called: what we might call the 'unique thumbprint'. It is about embodying
and communicating that vision to others. It is about being a 'keeper of the vision'
when there are obstacles to overcome or there is opposition to that vision
becoming a reality. It is about reviewing and renewing the vision, because there
will be mistakes along the way, with consequent mid-course corrections to
navigate. The King James Version of Proverbs 29.18 reads:

> Where there is no vision the people perish.

Although the New International Version translation is somewhat different,
the impact is equally powerful:

> Where there is no revelation, the people cast off restraint.

## What is vision?

> You cannot lead others on a physical journey, if you are unable to see;
> as Jesus said in a proverb he quoted: 'If a blind man leads a blind man,
> both will fall into the pit'.[1]

Let me offer a deliberately eclectic mix of definitions that have been a help to
me as I have sought to exercise visionary leadership in different contexts – inner
urban, suburban, rural, and now as warden of the Lee Abbey Community and
Conference Centre in Devon:

- 'The insight into the possibility of change and the potential that is there.'
  Senator Robert Kennedy

- 'A picture of the future that produces passion.'
  Bill Hybels, Senior Pastor, Willow Creek Community Church, Chicago

- 'A vision highlights the discrepancy between the present and ideal conditions and provides people with something to strive towards.'
  Attributed to *The Complete Idiot's Guide to Leadership*[2]

Vision comes out of the desire to enter into God's plans for his people and to learn to see clearly as God sees. There needs to be an element of dissatisfaction about the present so there can be the capacity to think with boldness and courage, daring to reach out and discover God's will for the future. True God-given vision, as opposed to jumping on the latest spiritual bandwagon or flavour of the month, is often difficult to attain. It is to the 'how' of discerning and developing vision that I now want to turn.

## Knowing yourself

It is vital to possess a degree of self-knowledge and understanding. We all bring to a new context a certain amount of personal 'baggage' – our own personal histories, both in general terms, in terms of life experiences and through what has shaped our Christian journey and ministerial role so far. This might well include the relationship we had with our training incumbent or equivalent in the 'probationary' situation. It is therefore important to know what your particular gifts and strengths are and to be aware of the weak areas. You also need to be clear about the values, assumptions and expectations that undergird your leadership style. Some kind of self-evaluation exercise, carried out individually or shared with someone else, will pay dividends as part of preparing to seek and share a vision with a congregation.

## Knowing your context

It is also vital to understand at an early stage as much as possible about the context within which you will minister (for further reading on this see pages 121–55). If you and others are to discern as accurately as possible the vision God wants to communicate, knowing the contours of the environment is an integral part of the process. This means having a working knowledge of the geographical area in which you are placed and the people who live there. (I am aware that for some readers the 'network society' of which we are now a part may mean that this may not be particularly relevant. However, though networks are of increasing significance, they have not yet replaced neighbourhoods, and the Church of England still remains committed to neighbourhoods. In this transition time it may require a 'bifocal ministry'.)

Understanding the history of the Church(es) is also vital, because that will shape not only present attitudes to what it is to be church, but also people's capacity to think towards the future. Whatever the context, questions need to be asked. Has the Church been a focus for unity or had a history of division? If there is a cluster of parishes, how did their coming together happen? Was there consultation locally, with deanery and diocese? Or was the union imposed, consequently leaving a lingering sense of resentment? What is the past history regarding the ministry of previous clergy? Issues like how long they stayed, what their styles have been, whether a vision has been 'cast' or whether a ministry has been essentially maintenance of the status quo need to be considered. Are there 'skeletons in the cupboard' which have caused loss of confidence in clergy, or has the overall picture been one of good, caring, collaborative and visionary leadership? Ridiculous as it may sound, such wounded history can live on through the generations, and if we are not aware of it and where necessary prepared to bring things into the open and seek healing, it will limit any significant outworking of fresh vision.

In a new situation there may be a strong temptation to rush towards discerning and communicating a fresh vision, but I believe that first playing the role of historian and analyst will always be time well spent. If this does not happen, it can lead to a lot of frustration and sometimes misinterpretation on the part of either clergy or congregation. This early part of the process can also incorporate acknowledging and celebrating the faith and faithfulness of people, especially where they may have had little or no encouragement from previous leaders, as well as perhaps setting the scene for an act of corporate repentance for any kind of wounded history.[3]

Along with seeking to understand the general and ministerial environments, making it a priority to get to know colleagues in more than a 'Hello, how are you?' way is also very important. By colleagues I include clergy, serving or retired, churchwardens, Readers and any others who have an identifiable leadership role. They will have insights from their greater and longer knowledge of the situation. In my experience, since they will be key allies in any changes that a fresh vision will bring about, asking them questions and valuing them for who they are as well as the roles they fulfil is again time well spent. Another dimension of this, whether in a formal or informal ecumenical situation, is to build good relationships with fellow ministers and priests. This is important not least because part of the vision-capturing process is to understand the unique purpose for each of the churches in the area, so there can be a collaborative rather than competitive approach. Discovering other church leaders' vision for ministry and what makes it distinctive can only be positive for the sake of the life and growth of God's kingdom.

In my experience, having held both parochial and diocesan posts, in most situations there are three groups of people. There are those who, when someone new is appointed, are desperate to see change, especially if what has gone before has, in their judgement at least, been less than church life in the twenty-first century ought to be. At the opposite end of the scale there are those who are fearful of any change, particularly if it is likely to reflect badly on the previous incumbent or others who have exercised leadership in the past. The middle ground is held by those who do not have the strong feelings of either of the first two groups – they will wait and see which way the wind blows!

## Where to start

When I moved from curate to vicar, I was given a piece of advice which I have, in turn, passed on to many others, including those who have been my curate colleagues. It sounds deceptively simple, but has proved to be invaluable. It concerns how to begin well, and how to pace changes that may need to be made in connection with any new vision and direction for the Church. The advice I was given was that on my first Sunday I should articulate those three possible positions outlined above, make people aware that I was sensitive to them, and go on to say that in the first six to nine months I would make no major changes (note the word 'major'). Having begun to understand something of the history of the area and of recent church life, and having got to know others in key positions of leadership, I would then meet with the church council to share my impressions of the strengths and weaknesses of the church as I saw them and invite their comments. That would then give us a basis on which to seek God's vision for the future. Having done that in three very different contexts I have to say that the advice given was brilliant. It reassures the more impatient that things are not going to drift; equally it encourages the more fearful that the new broom is not going to sweep everything familiar and valued out in the first six weeks, and then impose his or her five-year-plan. Those in the middle are reassured too, because there will be time for them to weigh things up in the light of the new leadership.

## The consultation process

Capturing a vision that is God-given has to be a collaborative process. This is not to abdicate responsibilities that are rightly invested in those called to lead, but as one bishop said at a new minister's licensing: 'Don't think you're God's only gift to the parish!' Having played the role of historian, the analyst aspect of leadership now needs to come to the fore. After a few months of having been in the parish, one approach to fulfilling this role could be asking questions such as:

'Why do we exist? How in one sentence would we describe who we are and why we are here? Imagine the church in 5 or 10 years' time. What will it look like, what impact will it be having?' This approach is known as 'vision building'. A similar exercise, sometimes described as 'horizon mission methodology', involves getting a church council or joint church councils – even the whole congregation – to undertake a 'past, present and future exercise' over perhaps half a day. Those involved are divided into small groups and invited first to reflect on the past, and identify both positive and negative features of church life over recent years – in some instances it might be five years; in other situations a longer perspective of 10 to 20 years might be more appropriate. Participants come back together and share their insights, and then move on to think about the present – What is encouraging? Where are the areas of growth? And, conversely, where are the weaknesses? In a changing situation they might also ask what improvements could be made. It needs to be said that 'pot shots' at particular individuals past and present are not permitted. This exercise is about 'us together reflecting on what kind of church we are called to be'. The final stage is to look to the future, to dream some dreams – 'if money and personnel were unlimited, what would we like to see our church become and be doing in 5, 10, 20 years' time?' Once more a sharing of insights takes place. Having carried out such an exercise in a number of different situations, I have been amazed by what has emerged and how new possibilities begin to be contemplated where before there may have been little or no vision.

When seeking a sense of direction for a church is a completely new concept, a helpful shorter and simpler exercise is to present the group with a document headed, 'What are we in business for?' A significant number of possibilities are offered, from which people are asked to choose the five most important, and out of those to see if they can identify one in particular that should shape the church's priorities. Examples of the options might include 'to provide moral guidance'; 'to maintain a Christian presence in a multi-faith area'; 'to share Christ's love in word and action'; 'to model a counter-cultural prophetic lifestyle'; 'to fulfil the two great commandments'. Whenever I have seen this particular approach used, no one has selected 'to raise money for the upkeep of the church' or 'to maintain the traditions of the church' as being the church's calling and priority, even though they have been included in the options. Through feedback and reflection on this exercise, people themselves begin to realize that priorities might have to change, and church council agendas would need to look different, in order to fulfil what they have begun to discover are pointers for a new direction.

'Future mapping' is a methodology originally developed by Bill Phillips, who was a management consultant with International Training Services. It invites us to use the power of imagination to engage with the future. This approach provides a different but potentially fruitful way into the process of discerning fresh direction and vision. Recognizing that the task of discernment can be a challenging process, this approach invites us to picture a staircase, which we can either view from the bottom or the top. It can be exhausting simply thinking about the climb up, and the obstacles to be surmounted. That can be the reason why many churches and their leaders get no further than thinking about or talking about the need for vision. However, if we stand at the top looking back from the perspective of having achieved our objectives, and noticing where we have come from and the path we took to arrive there, the perspective is rather different.

The church council or equivalent body is invited to imagine it is, say five years from now, and from the top of the stairs perspective, speak as if it is that date. They describe, in the present tense, the 'current' situation of the church – for example: 'the new church hall we have needed for years was opened two years ago, and two thirds of the money required was pledged at a Gift Day four years ago'; 'we now have six home groups, where five years ago there was nothing except one Sunday service for people to meet together; this all started with an "Alpha" course, that in turn led to a "Beta" course, which formed the basis of two home groups, and since then we have run an "Alpha" course each year.' The church council goes on to describe in more detail the steps by which they have reached that point. I realize this could sound rather contrived, but having used this method myself in different situations, and seen the benefits that others have gained by using it, I value it as an approach that has enabled some genuine 'future mapping'. It helps people to see what they might need to let go, and what would need to be put in place to see this preferred future realized.

## Communicating the vision

Whichever approach is used in the historian and analyst part of the process, the time then comes when, in the light of that contextualization and consultation, the new or renewed vision has to be shared with the church or group of churches for which you are responsible. In the gap between, a number of things need to take place if the vision is to be appropriately communicated and owned: to start with, some teaching and group work – especially for those in leadership roles, but preferably for everyone in the church – on the principles of God-given vision, can help people understand and embrace the concept more effectively. If this is not in place already, it is vital to call the church to prayer to seek God's direction. This can happen both in the Sunday services and through other specific opportunities that could be established.

The minister alone, or a small group of people with leadership responsibilities, will in my experience benefit from setting aside time, preferably 'off site', to reflect on the material and information that has been gathered. This gives an opportunity to listen to God, and begin to shape a response that can be set first before the rest of the wider church leadership, and then before the church or group of churches as a whole. This is not a matter of 'going up the mountain' and returning with tablets of stone around which there is no negotiation. If that happens, the vision remains solely the product and property of those who have been involved up to this point, and there will always be a sense in which it was felt to be imposed on others. Rather, out of a time of stillness and attentiveness to God, where his wisdom and insights are sought, you and the other leaders can come back to the people with what has been understood so far of God's vision for the immediate and longer term future, and together, the defining and refining process can continue. Sometimes that vision can come all of a piece and all at once, but I suspect this is rare. More often it is like pieces of a jigsaw puzzle coming together over time.

Leaders, therefore, do need to exercise their leadership gift, but the people for whom they are responsible must also take ownership. In my experience, this cannot be rushed or pushed – there must be plenty of opportunities for discussion and feedback. Emerging ideas can be shaped, developed and built on by encouraging others to offer suggestions, and bring their questions and even criticisms. This stage, I would suggest, needs to be a mixture of informal and formal processes. When the new possibilities begin to be shared, as leaders we can start asking, without being indiscreet or inappropriate, 'What if . . . ?', 'How would you see . . . ?', or 'I'm wondering if . . . ' kinds of questions in the ordinary conversations we have with people. Equally, it is quite likely that people will raise their questions with us, and this is a vital part of the process if there is to be true ownership. Along with the informal opportunities, the embryonic vision needs also to be shared more formally first with others in leadership – the full staff team if there is one, churchwardens, readers, PCC standing committee, church council – and in due course, with the whole congregation.

This process of communication and ownership is a sensitive one, and the leader can sometimes feel frustrated that it is taking longer than seems necessary!

As George Barna has put it:

> Most of the people interviewed agreed that the vision itself is probably not from God if it does not excite you to the point that you occasionally find yourself being impatient with people, systems and situations.[4]

This is because part of the almost indefinable gift entrusted to leaders and the reason they are in that position is to be able to 'see' a different future and, in practical terms, they have lived with the new possibilities longer and more closely than other people. It is important to communicate the vision in a way that is compelling and attractive, so that the fire can be lit in the hearts and minds of others. People will come to own the vision by evidence leading to conviction and not simply by persuasion. They need to be captivated by something of the excitement and possibilities that the leader has already begun to grasp.

## The emotions of change

Awareness of the 'emotions of change' is also a key part of this process of communicating the vision. In most churches there will be a small group, probably between 5 and 10 per cent, who if there are potential new developments and directions arising out of the new vision will take little convincing. They are the 'creators', people who like new ideas, being 'on the edge', risk-takers. Then there might be another 10 to 20 percent who like to see and be part of something fresh, but want to know that what is 'on offer' is practicable and workable. These are the 'progressives'. Importantly, this group often has the capacity to influence others who may be less sure. Between 25 and 40 per cent of many churches are 'builders' – people who have their questions, who can sometimes seem to get caught up unnecessarily in the details, but whose questions can often take a good idea and make it even better. A similar percentage are those who could be described as 'foundationals' – they positively appreciate the past and can be quite fearful of the unknown. Finally, there are the 'anchors' – looked at positively, they help retain the heritage of the past, but they can be not only fearful of anything new, but also sometimes negative and resistant. Recognizing that there will be these 'emotions' around is not only helpful in understanding where people are 'coming from', but also it will prepare you for the inevitability of some opposition. This does not mean that you and others in leadership have somehow got things wrong as far as the emerging vision is concerned.

Writing in 1975, Marris highlighted the central issue for reformers attempting to get their innovations implemented:

> No one can resolve the crisis of reintegration on behalf of another. Every attempt to pre-empt conflict, argument, protest by rational planning, can

only be abortive; however reasonable the proposed changes, the process of implementing them must still allow the impulse of rejection to play itself out. When those who have the power to manipulate changes act as if they have only to explain, and when their explanations are not at once accepted, shrug off opposition as ignorance or prejudice, they express a profound contempt for the meaning of lives other than their own. For the reformers have already assimilated these changes to their purposes, and worked out a reformulation which makes sense to them, perhaps through months or years of analysis and debate. If they deny others the chance to do the same they treat them as puppets dangling by the threads of their own conceptions.[5]

The received wisdom is that the process I have been describing of the vision being shared, understood and owned rarely takes less than a year, and can often take two. It seems we generally overestimate what can be achieved in one year, but underestimate what can be achieved in five. It means taking the medium to long-term view, and recognizing that it is better to take longer and get the majority of people on board, than rush things through in six months and find they 'jump ship'. People need to come to the point when they can truly say that the direction for the church encapsulated in the new vision is not 'his' or 'hers' or 'theirs' but 'ours'.

## Goals and objectives

The ownership process can be further assisted by the recognition that vision needs to be translated into specific goals and objectives. Such goals need to be right both for the church and for the time. Hopefully there will be congruence about these if accurate preparation and groundwork has taken place, but time scale and resources are sometimes where people come unstuck. It is helpful, therefore, to see goals as being divided into those that are:

- long term – 5 to 15 years ahead;
- medium term – 2 to 5 years ahead;
- short term – weekly, monthly, quarterly.

Whatever the specific time frame, it is vital that long-term goals, concerned with the overall direction of the church, are settled first. Medium and short-term goals need to fit in with the long term, and are taken on board only in so far as they help to advance the long-term objective.

Long-term goals themselves are of two main kinds. There are those which are specific and limited in scope, but may take time to accomplish.

There was a church that for over 40 years had been pouring money into an old two storey church hall. It was evident to everyone that this was not good stewardship, the building was unpleasant and unwelcoming and also limiting for new initiatives that the church wanted to take. However, because of the money that had already been committed to it, along with sentimental attachment, the nettle of replacing it had not been grasped.

A new vicar arrived, quickly realized that something had to be done, assessed the situation over the first year of his incumbency, and then began to talk informally about what might be achieved if the old building was demolished and a new facility built. During that period he also consulted others who had been involved in similar building projects, and asked a clergy colleague to share with the church council his church's experience, including how the financial challenges were met. Gradually, over the succeeding months, a picture was painted of a 'preferred future', and a decision taken unanimously by the church council to demolish the old building, sell the land and build something new adjacent to the church. There were many other hurdles to overcome, but the final encouragement to go forward was when, at a Gift Day, half the required money was given or pledged for the new building. The amount given was ten times more than any previous Gift Day had realized. The building was completed within two years of the new possibilities being shared, with the outstanding finances coming in over the next six years.

The other kind of long-term goal is one that determines the overall purpose and direction of the church for a period of time ahead. In contrast to one that is limited in scope, the longer the time span, the more general and the less specific this will be. To illustrate from an Old Testament example, the vision given to Abraham (then Abram) was quite imprecise:

Leave your country, your people and your father's household and go to the land I will show you. (Genesis 12.1)

There was a new overall direction for Abraham and his family, but only as he journeyed by stages through the Negev desert did things slowly become clearer (see Genesis 13.14-17 and 15.17-21) and then there were significant hitches and tests along the way.

It is important to say, however, that even if I am talking here in more general terms, this does not mean vague and unfocused. The long-term direction must be clear and compelling enough to keep the church on course in order to cope with potential short-term distractions. It is about clarity of overall direction, but with an open-endedness leaving plenty of room for the Holy Spirit's surprises. Or as a friend of mine put it: 'plans pencilled rather than inked in'.

## Mission and vision statements – their importance and purpose

Such long-term directional goals can be expressed in what is often called a 'mission statement'. I know some church leaders are resistant to this concept because we seem to trip over them wherever we go – in doctors' surgeries, post offices, schools or supermarkets. My response to this is that as a Church whose distinctive callings are worship and mission, our Scriptures are full of 'mission statements', even if they are not called such. Our Lord's 'summary of the law' in the two great commandments is one example; what is often referred to as 'the great commission' at the end of St Matthew's Gospel might be another. St Paul's own personal mission statement can be found in the words of his defence before King Agrippa:

> I will rescue you from your own people and from the Gentiles. I am sending you to open their eyes and turn them from darkness to light and from the power of Satan to God, so that they might receive forgiveness of sins and a place among those who are sanctified by faith in me. So then King Agrippa, I was not disobedient to the vision from heaven. (Acts 26.17-19)

These statements summarize what individuals and communities of God's people are called to be and do – they shape their response, they give direction and purpose.

Furthermore, having gone through a process of seeking to discern God's vision, it can help to have a statement that acts as both a summary and a description of a church's purpose and direction. This acts too as a benchmark against which to judge whether the decisions we take or activities in which we engage are fulfilling or furthering that vision.

Another potential area of confusion or concern can be the lack of agreement as to the difference between 'mission statements' and 'vision statements'. In *The Power of Vision,* George Barna defines a 'mission statement' as a broad-based philosophical statement about what the church is called to be and do. Thus many churches or organizations might even share a similar statement, a sentence or two capturing the essence of their calling and purpose. Here are some examples: 'to know Christ and make him known'; 'This church exists to be the people of God, through faith in Jesus Christ, in the power of the Holy Spirit, worshipping him, making disciples and serving others'; 'we believe we are called to be Christ-centred people, committed to his Church, concerned for his world.' In my own current context, the mission statement of the whole Lee Abbey Movement is 'Communicating Christ through relationships'.

A vision statement by contrast is specific and distinctive for a particular church or organization. It sharpens the focus of a mission statement and is much more detailed, specifying the direction the church will take and enabling it to concentrate on what it has been uniquely called to accomplish. It could be said to represent God's 'unique thumbprint'. So under the overall mission statement outlined above which is common to all aspects of the Lee Abbey Movement, we have a threefold vision statement here in Devon:

- to build community;

- to be God's welcome;

- to renew and serve the Church.

A mission statement can last a lifetime, but a vision statement is likely to need reviewing and adjusting as needs and opportunities change, and this is a natural and healthy progression for any church or organization.

## Sustaining the vision

In the last part of this chapter, I want to address the issue of sustaining a sense of vision and direction, because, like it or not, vision has a tendency to 'leak' and values to slip. It can be so frustrating to have done all that I have outlined above and possibly more, and perhaps several years on, find that people are still not focused on 'the main thing'.

### Potential limiting factors

I believe there are three main reasons that vision is hard to sustain: success, failure, and the pressures of everyday life and ministry. *Success* can mean that options multiply. Following a sharing of fresh vision the church grows numerically, size inevitably increases complexity, and complexity can confuse vision. I have seen a number of churches becoming outwardly successful organizations where everyone is busy, but connection with the overall vision and purpose has been lost.

*Failure* can also inhibit vision being sustained. If part of the strategy fails, some people at least are tempted to suggest it must have been the wrong vision. As leaders we can also give ourselves a hard time, taking the blame for whatever it is that did not work out. There needs to be the recognition that we will not 'get it right' every time. To quote another book title by Russ Parker, we need to be 'free to fail'. In fact failure can be a crucial stage on the pathway to new effectiveness.

> Failure is the drastic surgery God sometimes has to use to cut the stubborn nerve of self-sufficiency in a leader's life.[6]

Specific plans and strategies can always be changed and improved, leading to refinements over a period of time.

---

**A church embarked on a major fundraising campaign in order both to improve their facilities, and to take on more paid staff to further their work. It was an almost complete disaster, in that very little money came in and people were consequently demoralized and confused. One person was bold enough to say to the vicar, 'Do you think God is trying to tell us something?' She was clearly implying that since the plan was not working, then the vision for the church must be fundamentally wrong. The vicar was convinced that the overall vision was right, so his reply was, 'Yes, I think God is trying to tell us something – our approach to the fundraising has been wrong, and we need to acknowledge that, look at other approaches, and start again.'**

---

In other words, because a particular part of the plan does not work out, that does not mean there is a need to scrap the original vision.

Perhaps the greatest force that militates against vision being sustained is *life itself*. Vision as we have seen is about the 'big picture', a 'preferred future' for the church's ministry and mission; life, by contrast, is about this minute, and later on today. In ministry terms it is about having enough people to fulfil the tasks of this week, enough money to pay for the roof repairs never mind the ever-increasing diocesan quota. It is about the hospital visits that need to be made, the funeral that has to be prepared for and taken, the paperwork that was due in last week. In personal terms it is about our family needs, especially where there are young children or elderly parents to be cared for; the housework; personal health issues and financial pressures. No wonder that vision 'leaks'. The urgent and quite legitimate needs of today can cause us to lose the big picture.

## Keep on communicating

Recognizing these realities, is there anything we can do to counter this tendency? Something I have come to realize is that when as leaders we think we have overdone the communication of the vision, and in all honesty are ready to think about something else, we are probably just about getting through to the majority of people. Research tells us that a person needs to hear the same piece of information at least four times before they begin to grasp it, let alone remember it. Communication needs to be repeated over and over again. Not the same thing in the same way, but the substance needs to be repeated in fresh and creative ways.

> Having realized this, three years or so after my arrival in my last parish, following a major vision and commitment process which led to some fairly significant changes, I began to use the Annual Parochial Church Meeting not only as an opportunity for looking back over the past year, but to cast vision for the coming year. I learned to make the most of the opportunity presented by a meeting that we are required to have by law, but which has the potential to be quite dull, and often poorly attended. Building on that, in the early autumn, we began to hold congregational meetings both to see how things were working out in the vision process and as a further reminder, before we got too immersed in the autumn programme, of the overall purpose and direction of the church. This time of year seemed to be good for such a meeting, when there was some fresh energy after the summer break. Some of the ground was of course familiar to many in the congregation, but little harm is done in reinforcing the message. For others it was an important time to strengthen what may have become a vague recollection. For newcomers to the church it was completely fresh, and though it might take time for them to grasp the full implications of what was being communicated, at least they gained a sense that the church had some vision.

Communication in a growing church is a never-ending process. What I also found helpful was that having initially done most of the 'up front' vision-casting myself, gradually over the years others shared in the presentations which were offered in a variety of ways and that in itself helped the sense of ongoing ownership of and commitment to the vision.

### Variety is the key

As with the earlier part of the process, this task of sustaining the vision can be carried out informally, as well as in the larger and more 'formal' settings. It might be over a cup of coffee when you are visiting one of the lay leaders, or even better when you take them out to lunch. Or it might be at a church council day away, through a monthly magazine article or the weekly news sheet. Ask yourself, as you think about that vicar's letter slot, 'How vision-orientated is my writing?' We tend to think that such a slot is for something devotional, and of course there is a place for that, but it is also an opportunity to remind people of the church's purpose and vision. Increasingly, some church leaders use e-mail for doing this. What we are seeking is something that will come alive and stay alive in people, a passion that will motivate them to contribute their time, their gifts and the financial resources to make the vision possible.

## Celebrating success

Finally, it is important to take opportunities to celebrate the vision, especially when major steps forward have been accomplished. As a leader, especially when involved in building projects, I have found the Old Testament book of Nehemiah to be an inspiration and source of encouragement. In chapter 12 we read that when the walls had been rebuilt, Nehemiah organized a party for all the inhabitants of Jerusalem, within which specific people were mentioned and thanked for the part which they had played in the rebuilding of the walls. It is so important, both spiritually and psychologically for the people of God to celebrate the fulfilment of vision, a project becoming a reality. It may be that the whole task has not yet been completed, but it is still good to celebrate achievements along the way, especially when there have been significant setbacks and disappointments, as was the case with Nehemiah. I want to urge you as a leader to celebrate the initiatives and risks that have been taken, the sacrifices people have made, the generosity that has been shown, and the hard work that has been put in. If we take time to thank and honour people and celebrate achievements, it will help to ensure that the momentum to implement the ongoing vision will remain.

Here at Lee Abbey, having completed a new youth and outdoor centre costing almost £2 million, in addition to the formal opening ceremony we held a party in the new premises. There had been many challenges, frustrations and setbacks along the way, but when the building was complete and the contractors had left the site, it was wonderful to be able to celebrate. Nothing gives definition to vision like celebrating success.

## Vision – a work in progress

What is both exciting and challenging about leadership is that the task is never done. The vision God gives is never fully and finally implemented. In the light of this I have come to see that it is the compass, rather than the map approach to direction, which is more appropriate. The route on a map may look like a straight line, but the actual journey is rarely like that. It is more like a series of stops and starts, with mid-journey adjustments around obstacles. Leaders who use a compass rather than a map know exactly what the overall direction is, but can also cope with the unexpected and unpredictable. If as leaders we can live through these challenges and keep our focus on the destination and not just on the day's agenda, then there is more likelihood that our people will do so too.

# 6

# Mission

## The parish as a vehicle for mission

Philip North

### Introduction

At a training course for new incumbents in the North of England, one young priest was growing increasingly frustrated as he listened to the speaker. Eventually his frustration got the better of him, and he intervened furiously into the debate. 'We've got so much to do already!' he said. 'We've got services to organize, PCCs to chair, buildings to worry about and synods to attend. We've got school assemblies, home communions, funerals, weddings, baptisms and pastoral visits, and now on top of all this you expect us to do mission as well.'

This is a not uncommon attitude to the ministry of evangelism. Many experienced priests think of it as a bolt-on, or an extra clause in the job description (if one existed!). And because it is seen as an additional task, it is very easy to make it an area of planned neglect. 'We'll think about mission when we've mended the roof', is the way many think.

There are, however, two big problems with this attitude. The first is that it conflicts with Jesus' ministry and teaching, because constantly he sends his followers out to share the Good News of the kingdom and his very last instruction to them is to 'make disciples of all nations'. The second problem relates to our definitions of mission and evangelism. Mission is usually understood as our sharing in the whole of God's work of reaching out in love to his world. Within that wider picture, evangelism is the process (or processes) by which individuals respond to God through the commitment of faith and through becoming disciples. If our definition of mission is so broad, it is impossible to conceive of an ecclesiology in which these aspects of the Christian life are anything other than integral. Mission is not simply another activity which the Church decides to undertake. It is what the Church is because it is what God is.

But what does this mean in practical terms for the parish priest? It means that to be serious about the ministry of evangelism, we don't need to *do* more things, we just need to think differently about what we are already doing. We need to be aware of the evangelistic dimension of all church life, and be fairly brutal in our approach to those activities where the evangelistic dimension is hard to find. In his book, *Natural Church Development*, Christian Schwarz speaks of growth as the natural condition for a church, as it is for a plant.[1] If a church is failing to grow, the question should not be, 'So what extra do we do to encourage growth?' but rather 'What things are preventing growth?' There is much that is insightful in this analysis. A growing church is not necessarily a busy church. It is a church that has a clear vision and which has thought through and acted on its priorities.

In the rest of this section I will seek to identify evangelistic priorities in the everyday aspects of church life.

## Organizing missionary worship

One moment at a recent Youth Pilgrimage to Walsingham will remain with me for ever. We were celebrating the Eucharist with 800 teenagers in a big marquee. A group of youngsters had just danced in carrying huge bowls of incense which were placed around the altar. The priest in red vestments was whispering the words of consecration as the band played gentle music in the background. But it wasn't the action that captured me – it was the atmosphere. The assembled people were in total, awe-struck silence, every sense engaged in the worship of God. Nothing compares with those moments when people are suddenly lifted out of themselves by good worship. Nothing brings us more deeply into encounter with the mystery and majesty of God. Nothing is more truly evangelistic.

Worship is sometimes described as the church's shop window. What a mean and narrow definition that is. Worship is who we are. 'It is not the church that makes the Eucharist', Henri de Lubac has written, 'it is the Eucharist that makes the church.'[2] When we worship we are most fully ourselves as we are at unity with the only true reality which is the worship of heaven. Any attempt to engage a local church with mission and evangelism must begin with getting the worship right. Time spent planning worship is never time wasted.

Having said that, it is notoriously difficult to define what it is that makes for good worship. It is easy to assume that worship that matches our own particular taste or spirituality is bound to be what works, but this simply isn't the case. I have seen growth in churches that offer spontaneous charismatic worship and also in parishes that offer a very traditional High Mass. One of my friends in the Diocese of Durham saw extraordinary growth in a very down-at-heel church where he served as priest, and by far the most popular service was Prayer Book Evensong.

There are, however, some factors that can be identified, and the first seems to be that those leading worship have real confidence in what it is that they are offering. We do not need to explain or be embarrassed by the Church's worship. We just need to offer. The second is that a sense of community is achieved among those who are worshipping together. In this it is important that people are welcomed to worship and are given an opportunity to engage with their fellow worshippers afterwards, for example over a *good* cup of coffee. That sense of togetherness also needs to exist during the worship. There is nothing worse than going to a small church where 30 worshippers are spread across a huge nave struggling through long hymns, pitched too high. However if those worshippers are gathered together and sing something more appropriate to their ability, the worship can suddenly become electric.

Thirdly, the constant struggle for those who are organizing worship is to get the right balance between mystery and accessibility. On the one hand, we want people to be able to follow worship and know what they are doing. But worship that is over-explained can become banal and cringingly wooden. On the other hand we want people to encounter the mystery and transcendence of God, but if we do not give them the right pointers, they can end up confused and bored. This is a struggle that, as an organizer of worship, you will have to live with constantly. There are plenty of tips I could give: have good, clear orders of service with references to page numbers, make liberal use of times of silence, avoid the Anglican obsession with over-wordiness, keep notices and announcements to a minimum, only allow people who have the appropriate gifts to lead worship. But in the end it's all about developing a feeling for what is right. That means being open to the atmosphere of worship and sensitive to the thin line between engagement and boredom. It means having the courage to ask laypeople to feed back on your preaching or your liturgical style and the humility to act on what they say. And above all it means having the sheer nerve to let the Holy Spirit do the talking![3]

## Creating a learning community

Imagine a scenario. A young family have brought their child for baptism in your parish. They enjoyed the worship, they liked the feel of the church, they want to learn more about the faith they professed at the baptism. What do they do next? Where can they go to ask their questions and form the relationships that are such an essential part of discipleship?

For many centuries learning about the faith was what children did, but we are now in a situation in which there are three or four generations that have had no contact with the church or its teaching. In this context, it is of unparalleled importance that every parish has what the Bishop of Reading, Stephen Cottrell, calls a 'Maternity Ward' – a place where new Christians can be born. This would normally be a group comprising new and established Christians who meet together each week. The strength of this is that it recognizes that coming to faith is not so much about a reaching point of conversion as about an accompanied journey.

A few years ago I started using the *Emmaus* course in my parish in Hartlepool. I did it mainly because it was new and I'm a slave to fashion. However, it made the most tremendous impact over the years that followed with many new Christians being born and others discerning new ministries. We simply ran it again and again, because maternity wards never close. There are plenty of resources that can be used in a group such as this – *Alpha, Emmaus, Credo*. And research shows that home-grown courses are usually the most successful.

But it isn't only new Christians who need to learn. A healthy church is a learning community where all recognize that they are on a pilgrimage. On a recent visit to the United States I was struck by the way that most churches had a coffee hour or an adult Sunday School after the main service where there was teaching and discussion. And within this context, you as priest are not just teacher. You should also be head learner, making it clear to your people that you are on the same journey and ensuring there is time for you to study and grow in your own faith.

## Ministering 'to the edges'

You might be putting on the most glorious and sumptuous worship. You might be all ready to roll with an A1 Nurture Course. But still the church doesn't seem to grow. What is going on? Very often the problem can be that the agenda of the local church has become too domestic. It is so caught up with its own concerns and issues that it is failing to engage with the needs and issues of the community in which it is set. I remember a house church setting up in a very deprived area of Sunderland. People came in hordes from all over the North East, parking their flash cars in the high-security car park, but the church had no contact with the community who merely saw it as a legitimate target for stone-throwing youths. Then suddenly that church woke up. It realized that geographical context is not irrelevant, and its life was transformed as it set up an impressive series of community and youth projects.

We live in an age when words are not enough. Faith must be backed up by authentic Christian lifestyles. The huge Anglo-Catholic revival of the nineteenth century took place because priests and people expressed their faith in the Incarnation by feeding the hungry and clothing the destitute. So for us, all evangelistic ministry must begin by listening to the needs of our communities and by responding.

By definition, what this means in practice will vary according to the context. For some it will mean getting involved in community development issues and forming partnerships with other agencies. For some it will mean supporting local farmers and engaging with rural issues. For some it will mean helping to improve facilities for children or young people. Churches that grow are invariably those that are seen to have an active involvement in their communities and so where ministry is located at the edge.

Perhaps one or two examples will serve to clarify this.

---

The parish of St Chad's, Longton is in a deprived area of Stoke-on-Trent. The parish has always had an active ministry in the local schools, and realizing that there was nothing in the area for young people they set up a Sunday night Youth Club. Working with others they were then able to raise funds from Britannia Building Society and the Government's Children's Fund to employ a full-time children's worker who now runs after school clubs and groups for nearly 300 youngsters aged from 5 to 16. As well as serving the local community, there has been a big impact on the life of the church and recently 25 children were confirmed.

---

The parish of St Mary and St Peter, Sunderland, where I served as a curate, has a huge plant including large grounds and a hall. When I was there the grounds were overgrown and the hall was cold and dilapidated, but with a small and ageing congregation we lacked the resources to do anything about it. After I had left, the new vicar of the parish identified a need for office and meeting space within the local community. He formed a steering group comprising parochial church councillors and members of the local community and they managed to raise funds from the Church Urban Fund, the Single Regeneration Budget and local trusts. The hall is now a first-class community space and the grounds are a beautiful community garden. A building which used to be empty most of the time is now so busy that the vicar is able to keep the church unlocked, an oasis of prayer for the residents of a challenging community.

---

As priests it is vital that we take every opportunity to engage with those who are not part of our worshipping communities. The expansion of the church's ministry to schools since the 1988 Education Act and the Dearing Report[4] is a wonderful opportunity for this, and becoming known in local schools can very quickly bring about the situation where a priest is ministering not to a set of gathered individuals but to a community. Today the ability to deliver a good quality primary school assembly should be as integral to priesthood as preaching or taking a funeral. It is no longer any good saying, 'children aren't really my thing.' Make them 'your thing'!

Occasional offices are another God-given opportunity to engage with people outside the church. While the numbers of baptisms, church weddings and funerals are declining, it is still a significant gift that so many people come to the church to mark the major events of their lives. It is easy to be cynical about their motives for so doing, and tragically many priests are and neglect this area of ministry. If handled correctly however, the occasional offices can be a big area of growth. I met a priest in Walsingham a few months ago who had been sent to a desperately struggling parish in Liverpool where the congregation had declined to just 15. He now runs a flourishing church, and when I asked him how he had effected such a transformation he gave just one answer – baptism.

The birth of a baby is a point when many couples start thinking about the values with which they want their child to grow up, and many will turn to the local church for support in this. Churches need to have an agreed policy for the process that parents go through to prepare for their child's baptism, and experience shows that this is most effective evangelistically when it involves some degree of attendance at public worship. Nothing is ever achieved by selling the gospel short.

From our point of view, the all-important thing during the course of baptismal preparation is to enable relationships to be formed which run deeper than making a date for the baptism or handing over forms. Harnessing the talents of the laity is vital in this. Some churches have formed a baptism visiting team of people who agree to stand alongside parents during the course of the period of preparation. These lay people will welcome the parents to worship and help them to prepare for the baptism, for it is important that those who are taking the baptismal promises on behalf of a child know the significance of the words they are saying. They will also play a simple liturgical role in the baptism itself. Once good relationships have been formed, anything can happen, and while realistically most parents will disappear after the baptism, many will continue to attend worship and show interest in a nurture course.

I have always found marriage to be much more challenging from an evangelistic point of view (partly because I have spent so much time working in parishes where lots of people have babies but very few get married). However, once again the important thing is to make spaces where couples can get to know members of the congregation. Using laypeople in marriage preparation can help in this. In Hartlepool I teamed up with a neighbouring parish to put on a Wedding Preparation Day in the lounge of a local pub, and this gave us a wonderful opportunity to get to know the couples properly as well as giving some good input on the Christian understanding of marriage.

We need to show great sensitivity when using funerals as an evangelistic opportunity because it would be easy to take advantage of the emotional vulnerability of the bereaved. Nevertheless, many people ask deep and searching questions following the loss of a loved one, and we would be failing in our responsibilities if we did not answer these questions from a Christian viewpoint. I have always found that the best way to achieve this is liturgically. A simple invitation to worship can be issued by telling a bereaved family that their loved one will be remembered at church the Sunday after the funeral. There are also now some excellent liturgical resources for Services of Remembrance. By holding one of these every few months and inviting back the families of the recently bereaved, pastoral needs can be catered for in a way that is without pressure but allows opportunities to speak the gospel.

The decision to locate one's ministry at the edges can be a tough one for those congregations that are used to their priest being their personal chaplain. It requires good teaching, evolving patterns of lay ministry and some firm decisions on the part of the clergy, but the rewards are immense as the church over time builds up its fringe and makes contact with more and more members of its community.

## Making use of special events

In the past, when people spoke of 'mission' what they meant was 'having a mission'. I hope that I have demonstrated that taking evangelism seriously is not about putting on more events. It means thinking differently about what we already do and setting clear priorities. A missionary church does not necessarily hold missions, and indeed it would be irresponsible for a church to hold an evangelistic event unless it was already engaging with issues of mission across its whole life, but if the context is correct, holding an evangelistic event can be very significant for a local church. Indeed in many dioceses parishes are encouraged to organize a mission weekend as part of their annual programme of events along with harvest festival and the 'Summer Fayre'.

The most important consideration in planning an evangelistic event is to be absolutely clear about your aims. This means being specific about the group of people you wish to reach (for example parents of the recently baptized, members of a parents and toddler group, or residents of a new area of housing) and wrapping the event around the needs, interests or concerns of those people. It also means getting the follow-up right, and indeed thinking backwards from the follow-up to the event. For example it is no good holding a wonderful mission service and inviting people to come back if the service the following Sunday is interminably dull. Again there is no point in encouraging new people to explore the Christian faith if there is no nurture course where they can do that.

The other great benefit of events is the renewal of the existing congregation. An event such as a teaching week or school of prayer can bring new vitality to tired Christians. To my mind one of the best examples of this is 'Fan the Flame', a five-night teaching week, pioneered by Bishop Lindsay Urwin, that has the advantage of being organized entirely by a group of laypeople called by the incumbent. The same sort of renewal can be achieved by an event away from home. Pilgrimages to places such as Walsingham or the Holy Land and visits to events such as Spring Harvest or Greenbelt can have a remarkable impact on the lives not just of individuals but of whole churches.

## Conclusion

The recent Church of England report *Mission-shaped Church*[5] has encouraged us to think very radically about what new forms of church life might be emerging. We need to engage very seriously with the issues that this report raises. However, it would be ruinous if this meant that we were to write off what some people would call 'old church'. For the majority of people in this country their main contact with the church will be the parish with a building, a congregation and a priest, and the emergence of new forms of church life does not mean that this traditional model is dead. It is quite possible to see significant growth in churches of all traditions as long as priest and people have a confidence in the gospel and a burning desire to make new disciples. The key factor is to be aware of the evangelistic dimension of all that we do, and to do it well.

# Moving out: first steps in mission and evangelism

## Sue Hope

How do you, as a new incumbent, start thinking strategically about mission and evangelism in the parish? It is unlikely that this will be at the top of your list of priorities in the first year, and indeed, until you are acquainted with the character and personalities of church and community, it would probably be a mistake to do so. However, it is equally important to begin to *ask the questions* about mission within the first two years, before the church diary begins to 'harden up', and your mind is overtaken by church-based issues. By now, you will have realized that life in the parish has a curiously centripetal force – pulling everything 'inwards' towards the organization and maintenance of church life – and it can be the case that it requires real effort to think and plan 'outwards'. Recognizing this factor and then working at it – through prayer and through planning – is vital. It may even be that in the course of praying for and about mission, you discover a personal, in-built resistance to mission itself – fear of vulnerability, fear of failure, weariness – and that some of the essential work to be done is on this more personal level. That is why it is crucial for those in leadership to be clear that, with very few exceptions, we are all wearing 'L-plates' when it comes to planned thinking about mission.

In addition, for 1500 years the Church of England has been a settled, pastoral church, ministering to a culture that has been largely familiar with the Christian story and sustained by Christian symbols. That is no longer the case, and parish churches are beginning to realize that there is a fresh task ahead – that it is time to tell again, in word and in deed, the story of Jesus. For many, both clergy and laity, this is a new venture, a steep learning curve, and it helps to acknowledge this, both publicly and privately. As leader, you need to model a certain freedom to explore, to experiment, to evaluate and to fail if you and the congregation are to learn together how to become 'fishers of people'. Agreeing with the church that all are learners in this, and giving permission to fail can have a liberating effect upon mission activities, turning them from 'things we ought to do' into adventures with the Holy Spirit.

What follows are some suggestions for learners: principles and practices which have been worked out at the coal-face of parish mission. They are not exhaustive, and they are intended as springboards rather than strait-jackets. Many of them can be found in various and more detailed forms in other publications: all will benefit from further reflection and work.[6]

## Identify and build a core mission team

Mission and evangelism needs to be the fire in the Church's belly, rather than a bolt-on optional extra 'for those who like that kind of thing'. It is a bit like the furnace in a great liner, deep down in the bowels of the ship, fuelling its progress. At its heart, the church needs to be fuelled by the fires of compassion and of concern. One of the best ways of fanning that fire is to identify and work with a small mission team. The team may be PCC members, they may be those in the church who have been identified as having a special concern for the 'outsider', they may be the staff team – but their task is to generate heat concerning mission, to keep it at the forefront of the church's agenda, to be thinking 'next steps' and to be praying regularly for the mission task. It is not the task of the mission team to *do* the mission on behalf of the church, but to encourage, enable and equip others to do it.

## Be both Celtic and Augustinian

The Celtic mission was marked by a kind of 'free-flowing' responsiveness: the Irish missionary would embark on his journey across the Irish Sea in his coracle, believing that wherever the wind blew him was the place God had ordained for his mission. Augustine, on the other hand, landed at Kent with his team of 40 monks and together they planned the mission carefully, moving out, consolidating and then moving on again. Both the 'responsive' and the 'strategic' approach are valid models of mission and each will have its application in parish mission. It may be helpful to the incumbent to ask 'Which do I do naturally?' and 'Which does the church do more naturally: are we Celts or Augustinians?' and 'Should we try working at the one we do least naturally in order to redress the balance?' Put another way, this is very much a matter of 'right-brain'/intuitive activity or 'left-brain'/logical activity: both have their place in the Church's mission.

## Make the most of opportunities before setting up events

Mission events have their place. But they work best when the *culture* of the church is one of 'natural outreach' – when both incumbent and church members are alert to the daily opportunities to share something of the reality of the gospel with those with whom they come into contact. Unless this is a natural part of the church's life and self-understanding, outreach events will probably fall on stony ground and will lack integrity. They may, indeed, have the over-intense 'taste' of a plate of icing without any cake to give it real substance. Learning to see the opportunities is an important part of this process of natural outreach. We are reminded that instead of putting off mission by pushing it into an imaginary future, we are to 'lift up our eyes and see' that the opportunity is now, today

(John 4.35). It takes a certain mental and spiritual discipline, an alertness, an openness to the promptings and urgings of the missionary Spirit to respond to the moments and opportunities which he gives – and an acknowledgement that we suffer from a kind of will-to-not-see, a glaucoma of the spirit, the kind of chosen blindness that affected the two religious leaders in the story of the man who fell among thieves (Luke 10.25-37).

## Think 'micro-mission'

'Jesus sent them out two by two' (Luke 10.1). That is small in terms of mission.

> Two middle-aged women in Doncaster wanted to reach out to the young prostitutes in their area, most of whom were also heroin addicts. What could they do? They knew nothing about prostitution or about drugs. They made up two thermos flasks of coffee and took them out to the women on the street. That led to offering to pray for them by name and, in time, a ministry developed among them. There is now a 'shop-front' where the women can get health advice and support if they want to come out of prostitution – and some of them have come to faith. But it started with two flasks of coffee.

Similarly, 'micro' might apply to the numbers which a church is aiming to reach. It may be, for example, that the incumbent identifies four different men who happen to have been coming along to church for a few months, or three young women with children who have started to attend. Prayerfully considering what might be the next step to draw the four, or the three, into stronger relationship with the church, and then doing it, could prove very effective in terms of mission. Adding to the church through micro-mission can be more effective in the long run than laying on big events.

## Think in 'steps'

The leadership of the church is very often at full-stretch coping with the demands of ministry and it can be daunting to an incumbent or a church to contemplate 'mission': 'How on earth are we going to manage to do *more?*' Thinking in 'steps' can be useful, both in terms of the manageability of mission, and also as a way of trying to keep in step with the Holy Spirit. So for example: 'No one ever comes from *that* estate' is the received wisdom about 'Woodlands'. As a first step, the PCC have the Woodlands estate on their agenda each time they meet and for the first two meetings all they do is to stop and pray for the estate. The third time they meet someone suggests finishing the meeting early and then walking prayerfully and reflectively round the estate. At the next meeting someone has the idea of taking out a small Christmas gift with a card to each house. One or two good contacts are made through this and the next time the PCC meets they discuss how they might build on these. Taking small and manageable steps in mission can lead to growth without overwhelming the leaders.

## Targeting

Anglicans can be wary of the language of 'targeting' when it comes to specific groups, partly because of the inherited tradition that the Church of England is open to all. Of course, that remains so, but it is a fact that Jesus was not afraid to think in terms of 'people groups' (Matthew 10.5) and Paul clearly saw himself as the 'apostle to the Gentiles'. Setting targets will affect the overall policy of the church – deciding, for example, to concentrate *this* year on building up contacts with children up to the age of 8 and their parents, and young singles, and then *next* year to focus on bereaved people, or men between the ages of 20 and 45. Targeting does not exclude other people groups, but it does have the effect of focusing energy and of encouraging the leadership to be tactical, including in its financial commitments, and helps to be clear about what a leadership team is trying to achieve when planning an activity or event.

Targeting also makes events fit people, not the other way round. Often a local church will put a lot of effort into setting up and publicizing an event for those outside the church, only to find that few people actually attend. The result of this can be a disappointment and a sense that 'we're not very good at this'. A more fruitful way to engage in mission is to call to mind the actual people to whom the activity is directed, and to use them as a focus. 'We've got several young families on the fringes . . . what can we do as a next step to draw them into relationships with church families/introduce them to the church's leadership/present them with the challenge of the gospel . . . ?' is the kind of question that is likely to produce an appropriate event.

## Teamwork

Teamwork is essential in local church mission. Mission and evangelism are no longer the preserve of gifted individuals (though they need recognition and affirmation) but, increasingly, the task of the whole Body of Christ. Working as teams has practical advantages as well as theological credibility. For example, many people feel wistfully that they would love to be part of some kind of 'evangelistic enterprise' but feel they lack the experience or courage to evangelize on their own. Working in a team means that many gifts can be offered in the service of the gospel.

---

A local church recently laid on a women's coffee morning in a hotel. Some women made flower arrangements to decorate the tables, some ran a bookstall, some designed the publicity and invitation, others prayed. They found they could do in a team what they could not have done alone.

---

This has often been proved particularly helpful in men's outreach, where, for example, a church men's group may organize a walk, and a pub lunch and invite non-members along. Walking and talking together, in a relaxed and informal way, can be liberating for people who otherwise would not think of themselves as evangelists. Teamwork allows different interest groups and different age groups to engage in mission 'their way', to have a go, and to develop outreach in a way that is appropriate for them.

## Relationships are key

Running some kind of regular 'nurture course' has been seen to be an important part of contemporary mission.[7] The experience of those who have been using courses regularly is that the context is as important as the content. Whether a church runs *Alpha, Emmaus, Start!, Saints Alive* or *Credo*, the key factor which determines the success of the group is the quality of the relationships within it. It is probably true to say that, by the end of the course, those who continue into further life within the Christian family will most frequently be those who have made strong relationships with each other and/or with one or two church members. They have been 'caught' in the network of loving and committed relationships which ideally make up the Body of Christ. Careful investment into the quality of relationships in the Christian community is therefore an important factor in engaging in mission.

## The priority of prayer

It was John Taylor, a former Bishop of Winchester, who wrote that mission is about finding out what God is doing, and then joining in,[8] and learning how to interpret the Spirit, spotting the footprints of God in the earthiness of the ordinary life of a local community and following them into the unknown, is at the heart of true mission. Prayer is the most vital component of mission: prayer which is regular, sustained and, above all, intimate: a 'leaning on the heart of God' which produces a kind of attentiveness to the brokenness of the world, deep compassion and a massive and glorious quality of resilient hopefulness. Without prayer, mission becomes mechanical, strained, unlovely – with prayer, it finds itself to be an overflow of grace, natural, life-bearing and a deeply-joyful partnership with God.

# Mission and community

## Ann Morisy

Effective mission requires a commitment to be outward looking. It also requires the ability to maintain a consistent approach and to communicate to others within the church in such a way that they are enabled to play their part. Inevitably, exercising ministry within established denominations can involve wading through a host of bureaucratic demands and processes. The first challenge therefore in relation to mission is to find a way of keeping the demands of bureaucracy and the ecclesiastical structures in their place. This calls for clarity about priorities as well as finding a way of ensuring that pressing demands do not crowd out the important, but less pressing tasks.

There are two ways of ensuring a proactive approach to mission:

- Work out your own theory of mission.

- Actively involve the community.

In a nutshell, you need to have a rationale for doing the things you do and you need to explain that to others for them to be involved.

It is important to be able to articulate the theory of mission that forms the basis of your approach. This enables the congregation and others to know 'where you are coming from' and to understand why you want to do one thing rather than another. It links general, day-to-day actions with an analysis of the factors that can hinder (or foster) the flourishing of God's kingdom here on earth.

> An interesting example of how both analysis and response are essential components of a theory of mission is provided by the Church Growth Movement. Using evidence that culturally homogenous churches grow

faster than those that are culturally and demographically diverse, and that more people are reached by increasing the number of congregations rather than by building up a single congregation, the Church Growth Movement instigated a project called DAWN. This involved planting a congregation for every 2,000 in the population.

There are many different theories of mission. Each of us will have our own 'take' on the factors that affect the flourishing of God's kingdom, and consequently our personal theory of mission will involve different approaches and nuances. My own theory of mission has three elements:

1.  The importance of struggle for the flourishing both of the creation and of humanity;

2.  The mysterious part that those who are poor and marginalized play in the purposes of God, and in particular, the way they mediate an awareness of Christ (Matthew 25);

3.  The wide fraternal relations that follow from an awareness of the fact that we all share the same Heavenly Father.

These three elements provide the motivation to develop opportunities for people to participate in projects that involve them in taking struggle into their lives, often by working with and for people who live in poverty and others who have first-hand experience and knowledge of struggle.

Denominations are different in the freedom they 'allow' their ministers to maintain their own distinctive theory of mission. However, regardless of this, without a theory of mission it is hard to avoid drifting into populism, or traditionalism, or simply to drift.

---

When you consider your own theory of mission you will need to ask three fundamental questions:

*   Based on your analysis of the world today (or your context), what do you consider to be the three or four things that are really important in helping us move closer to the Kingdom of God?

*   What steps would help people to engage positively with the world in relation to these factors?

*   In your own context, how would you put these steps in place?

---

# Community involvement

Involvement in the community is essential if a church is to extend its contact beyond requests for baptism, weddings and funerals (now seriously declining in numbers). However, community involvement or community ministry can become an automatic response, a kind of catch-all solution. In particular we need to be aware of thinking only in terms of 'meeting needs'. This may be seen as placing the church and congregation in a position of superiority, implying that those who are needy are in some way deficient, while competence and resourcefulness are retained in the hands of the helpers. The gospel with its capacity to overturn everyday assumptions will have none of this. Jesus makes it clear that it is those who are needy who carry a potent transformational capacity. Furthermore, repeatedly focusing on needs can distract from a host of graceful kingdom dynamics that can be set in train when those who are secure, and apparently competent, encounter those who know the demands and limitations of a life marked by struggle.

Mission has to be about more than 'meeting needs'. It is important to understand a church's community involvement in terms of discipleship and hospitality:

- Community involvement when combined with a structure of participation (and this might only be a humble rota) enables lay people to embrace a more authentic expression of discipleship. The Catholic theologian Karl Rahner suggests that '*venturesome love*' is at the heart of discipleship. This view challenges the tendency for discipleship to be reduced to 'doing tasks in church'. Discipleship of the venturesome type is essential if a local church is to earn the right to speak of the gospel. Authenticity is one of the few values that still prevails in a postmodern context, therefore the local church and its members have to 'walk the talk'. Just as our postmodern context calls for new and fresh ways of being church there is an equally important need for new and fresh ways of expressing discipleship.

- Hospitality is one of the few themes consistently referred to in both Old and New Testaments and its centrality is endorsed by the Early Church. The offer of hospitality is one of those rare situations where the person most in control, the host, has all the obligations and the vulnerable or less powerful guest has almost all the rights. In giving hospitality the host must not try to change the guest, and must grant the guest the right to remain a stranger, accepting the possibility of no personal exchange or significant encounter between host and guest. This is a principle that applies equally to the church-run lunch club for elderly people, the drop-in for asylum seekers or for those with enduring mental illness or who are homeless.

The classic examples of hospitality indicate that often change may come about by the offer of free space. If we take the potency of grace seriously then hospitality offered generously and with an open hand will have a transforming impact.

- Participative discipleship and hospitality are particularly important today because evidence suggests that they are in ever shorter supply in neighbourhoods in Britain.

---

### Social capital

**Both community involvement and hospitality, in the sense of being open to and trusting in relation to strangers, are important aspects of social capital. Social capital refers to the trustworthiness of relationships within a neighbourhood and the degree to which support is extended beyond or restricted to one's own network. The radius of trust varies between neighbourhoods, and even between streets within a neighbourhood. When the level of trust between people falls it makes for heightened anxiety, and prompts the desire to move elsewhere. When people move away, their place is then taken by 'strangers', once again reducing the level of trust. The neighbourhood becomes less stable – and hospitality to others is eroded.**

---

- Where in your neighbourhood do you consider the 'radius of trust' to be the shortest? Is there a distinctive mission strategy you might adopt in relation to this area?
- What collaborative or joint action with other agencies in your neighbourhood might strenghten and sustain your approach to mission?

## Taking anxiety seriously

The chances are that if you are involved in ministry in an area of high mobility and little community participation then church membership is likely to be low. The loss of positive social capital over the last 30 years has been a significant contributory factor in the loss of energy in church life. It is not just increasing secularization that has affected church attendance. The fragility of community life in many neighbourhoods has had a profoundly negative impact on our churches. If we are to grow churches, we have to grow community, and in this way we also grow the kingdom of God.

Shrinking congregations and the loss of trust within neighbourhoods mean that the problem of anxiety has to be taken seriously. Anxiety affects us all. We are all inclined to organize our lives in ways that are designed to reduce anxiety levels. Anxiety is a negative emotion. It makes us unattractive. It makes us reactive or cold-blooded, rather than responsive. Anxiety can be a root cause of racism and the associated dynamic of scape-goating, because people are anxious they pick on those who are different. Anxiety can destroy communities. It can destroy churches and because high levels of anxiety can bring low resilience, it can destroy ministry

More than anything, anxiety can make individuals or groups unattractive to others. Few people are likely to join an acutely or chronically anxious group, so numbers decline increasing anxiety and creating a vicious circle. For this reason alone there are habits to cultivate and in which to coach others in order to reduce anxiety:

- Aim to reduce the 'voltage' that is in the (emotional) system. One of the most important ways of doing this is to model or demonstrate ways of containing our own anxiety. Being able to resist being provoked is certainly an asset in anxiety prone contexts, although this should not be confused with being 'laid back'.

- Be aware of your own reactive buttons. We all have buttons which when pressed can inadvertently put us on edge and trigger unwarranted reactions. Being aware of how you react to situations may give you the split second's grace that can transform reaction into response.

- Discipline both your head and your heart to recognize that problems have multiple and interrelated causes and be aware of the real danger of scape-goating.

- Try not to pick up other people's anxieties. Always make a distinction between listening to and hearing people's gripes and actually siding with them. Encourage people to take responsibility for their own feelings and come to their own decisions about what is best for them.

- Make use of humour and fun. This is surely one of the most delightful kingdom reversals. In anxious situations laughter is, to use Peter Berger's expression, a 'rumour of angels'.

- Aim to be a 'non-anxious presence'. This involves becoming adept at identifying your own anxiety, because only then will you have any chance of reducing it. If you can achieve this you will feel able to 'park' the anxiety and consciously put it away.

---

**Buddhists recommend softening the eyes as part of the quietening that helps us to be more open (to God) and each other. This may seem a rather obscure and even dubious approach to managing anxiety, but there is an extraordinary endorsement to the process: the most reliable way of softening what might otherwise be hard eyes is to look upon a new born baby and then without conscious effort our eyes soften – and our hearts moisten.**

---

# Mission: a perspective

## Anne Richards

A few years ago an elderly clergyman, whom I admired and respected, who bore his last illness with a resigned fortitude and impeccable dignity, died. Nothing so odd about that, you might think, but what made this death stay with me and haunt me still, is that just before he died, he told me he no longer believed in the promises of the Christian faith. He said that, facing his end, he no longer imagined there could be anything beyond death and that he had decided to lay down his faith, the history of his relationship and struggle with God. 'And oh, Anne,' he said, 'it is such a relief.'

The Christian vocation is given to us as a joy and a privilege. To be called into ministry is a gift, it makes us feel special, set apart, consecrated to God's service. But there's a flip side which I have seen increasingly at clergy meetings and conferences, where my dear friend's words have again risen to the surface. I have met people who, being filled with love for others, have given it all away and kept none for themselves or for their family. I have met people for whom the greatest torture is presiding at a funeral and hearing every word ring hollow. I have talked to beloved parish priests whose parishioners adore them but whose hearts are stone to a sense that what they have done is worth anything at all. Many of these clergy are struggling along the road with faith clinging about them as a terrible burden. The expectations, and perhaps especially the *mission* expectations of the Church weigh them down. They long to lay it down, they long for relief. Anything else – affirmation, a sense of value, a sense even of doing God's will, that is too much to hope for.

Much of this is our fault. The way we talk about what we must do in the Church, the expectations we have of missionary people, the results we are looking for, are huge. What is the end of mission? Is it a place where *every human person* has had the chance to encounter the Good News and be changed by it? Is it nothing less than the transformation of the *whole world*? Is it the bringing in and making evident *everywhere* the kingdom of God? These are vast visions and massive enterprises. The five marks of mission[9] and the mandate they carry are enormous, their implications fill up not just one lifetime but generations of obedient, loving, transformative work.

How can we ever live up to this call to partnership with God in this giant enterprise? We are given resources and materials, books and specialists – how to make all sorts of things happen, how to work for change, how to empower, how to sustain, how to turn around, how to build up. How exhausting and hopeless this task is for some parish priests, and how disempowering when your building is falling down and your congregation scarcely extends beyond the first pew.

We need to get some sort of a grip on what mission really is. In the first place in proclaiming the *missio dei*, the mission of God, we ignore the most important fact about it. We are *not* God. God calls us to partnership, sure, but not to give us impossible burdens, to test us to destruction. God calls us to exercise particular gifts in particular situations and *that* is our task. We have to give ourselves permission to call that task the mission of the Church for *us*. It can be a hard lesson to learn, especially when the prevailing pressure to build up the Church seems to weigh heavily upon us.

Secondly, human values about what is and is not worthy of the name 'mission' get in the way. Does God desire or respond to the big event more than the prayers of a disabled man? It is evident that the answer is 'no', but where does this get acknowledged? Small things matter to God. That time of prayer, that faithful worship of the few, that fierce love of a small insignificant church to a small insignificant community, surely these are all part of God's missionary vision for the reconciliation of the whole world to God's own self. Because that 'whole world', the whole creation, contains everything great *and* small. There just isn't enough affirmation of the small things, because we're taught to imagine that big is better and that success is about increase, the numbers game and prosperity.

Why on earth did Jesus tell the story of the widow's mite if not to challenge our perspectives of success, worth and value? What about his reaction to his disciples playing the 'who is the greatest' game? We listen to the media and not to our Lord.

Thirdly, clergy and congregations can collude together to prevent this powerful affirmation of doing little things well and to prevent anyone seeing that what is done actually contributes to the total mission of the Church. So huge amounts of energy are spent on planning, administration, envisioning, commissioning, doing new things, without pausing for one minute to find out what God is up to and has already done among us right here, right now. Sometimes ministry cuts right across the work of the Holy Spirit, not waiting to find out what God is doing and joining in, but relentlessly pursuing the dream which is only ours and therefore flawed. Mission is not about doing more and yet more, but about adding spiritual *depth* to what is done, so that others may look on it and see the reality and richness of a living faith held by people fully alive in Christ. Why else would anyone want to be a part of it? It is time to see the brilliantly varied pattern of mission available throughout Christian ministry and to affirm each thread as good, complete and of value.

Douglas Coupland used a striking image in his novel *Girlfriend in a Coma*,[10] where he described the whole of heaven cheering whenever we accomplish some tiny little thing. Just as we are filled with delight when a child totters a couple of steps, so heaven takes delight in anything we do which is oriented towards God in the obedience we owe. But we can lay burdens upon clergy equivalent to expecting wobbly toddlers to be mathematical geniuses.

I like to think that my dear friend's unbelief was cherished by God for the profound emptying out of his life in the service of others that it marked, so that in death he has been filled again and found indeed that his burden is light. The gift of lifted burden should be every Christian's heritage. It should be part of our mission thinking.

# 7

# Parish systems

Guy Wilkinson

## Leading, managing and administering in the parish

To many, especially those approaching incumbency for the first time, the tasks
of administration and management are burdens which seem increasingly to
outweigh the 'real' work of ministry. To others it is indeed the role of the vicar
to lead, manage and administer in such a way as to enable the gifts and ministries
of many others to be liberated and held together creatively and fruitfully. For
myself, I think it is possible and desirable to hold to the understanding that
'stewardship' is what brings together coherently these tasks of administration,
management and leadership and combines them with the more traditional
understanding of ordained ministry. To be 'stewards of the mysteries of God'
need not be a sacramental perspective alone.

## The working environment

To be a vicar, rector, priest in charge or team vicar is to have one of the least
institutionally structured roles in the professional world. Parish clergy are not
employed by anyone, being officeholders, and the range of management systems
within which most people work are either largely unknown to clergy, or exist only
on a voluntary basis. There are of course some formal requirements on parochial
clergy, such as presiding at the celebration of the Holy Communion on Sundays,
or chairing the PCC, but these are modest matters compared with the structured
requirements laid upon a teacher, doctor or company executive by their
professional standards or indeed by the law. The systems of training, preparation,
execution, evaluation and recording that are for most a standard part of being
employed are not required of clergy who are largely free to use their time as
they see fit. Although no doubt the views of PCC and churchwardens will be of
significance, clergy may prioritize their ministry very largely according to their own
individual assessment of what matters – and this may sometimes lead to a quite
low priority for administration and in some cases effectively to a near disdain for
administrative tasks.

Of course, this is not to say that systems for management and administration do not exist in the Church; increasingly they do, and organizations such as Administry and other consultancies have for many years offered real support and expertise. And of course there are many clergy whose previous experience equips them well for these tasks, and yet others who have equipped themselves since ordination, not least for some by tackling and achieving an MBA. Management of the business of the parish through the PCC and its groups, budgeting, quinquennials, Articles of Enquiry, taking part in one of the systems of ministerial review, dealing with employment issues, all these are part of the normal business of the parish priest. However they are not contractual conditions of employment, but rather a set of obligations taken on with greater or lesser enthusiasm and without the penalties for non-compliance that are likely to be visited on those who are within an employed structure.

Equally this is not to imply that your work load as a parish minister is less than it is for others. The demands of a parish, particularly the larger urban parishes or the extensive rural group ministries, on the parish priest can be enormous and can be greatly extended by the traditions of always being available to parishioners in need. Because we are engaged in vocational ministry, something to which clergy give their whole life, there are often none of the work/time boundaries that are in place to protect people in employed professions, although junior doctors and teachers might have something to say about their hours of work

There is a further factor that particularly distinguishes clergy work practice, which is that for most, the norm is to be the only paid full-time person in the immediate work environment. Of course, in an increasing number of parishes there are other paid work colleagues, whether these are other clergy in the context of a team ministry, or youth workers, community workers or parish administrators; and in every parish there is a team of voluntary colleagues, from self-supporting clergy, churchwardens and Readers through the whole range of those who give their time to the life of the local church. Nevertheless, your work context is likely to be very different from that of most people and from what you have been used to prior to ordination. For most people the work context is a team environment in which each employee is one of a significant number of other employees in the enterprise. Employees are organized into a structured system in which each has an allocated range of responsibilities within an overall authority structure. For clergy this is not the case and the normal working environment is much more solitary.

All of these factors lead to particular challenges for clergy in their way of working. So, how in the presence of substantial demands upon them, but in the absence of fully formalized structures for collegiality, authority and accountability, can effective ways of working be devised and maintained? How can you be true to your vocation to serve and yet find the appropriate place for the range of management tasks that have to be undertaken? How can you avoid becoming either the 'jack of all trades and master of none' or the priest who sets aside all tasks other than pastoral or liturgical as not being a valid part of your ministry?

## Learning from the wider world

First, it is important to recognize and accept that the role and context of parish clergy is particular and has real differences that distinguish it significantly from all other professions, and that in the context of the Church of England this is likely to remain the case. This is not because people in other roles do not have equivalent motivation and commitment; there are as many dedicated teachers, nurses, human relations directors and civil servants as there are clergy. It has much more to do with the historical, structural and cultural frameworks within which clergy minister and are likely to continue to minister.

But it is equally important not to draw the conclusion – as is too commonly the case – that clergy have little to learn from the secular world about how we may work most effectively. 'Management' is too often used as a derogatory term; proficiency in administration is too often belittled as being of secondary importance to pastoral tasks; clarity and decisiveness in human relations are too often referred to as impersonal or authoritarian. We do not have a monopoly on care and concern and we have much to learn from others about the systems and techniques that have been developed and applied over the years aimed at effective management and administration at the personal and corporate level. It is not without relevance that most of Jesus' parables and illustrations are drawn from the world of work, rather than from the religious context.

So don't be afraid or dismissive of learning from other professions; take an interest in how others do things and be ready to learn their techniques and to modify and adapt them as appropriate to our own contexts. The supermarket manager has much to teach you about how to get to know your parishioners; the public relations and advertising executives have much to teach about effective communication of the gospel; the general practitioner has much to teach about collective and collaborative working. I don't think it is unreasonable to acknowledge even that the professional human resources manager displays in practice more care of her employees by a rigorous insistence on clear working practices, on health and safety and even in managing redundancy than very many of her ecclesiastical equivalents.

It is precisely because your working context is likely to be very different from that of colleagues in other professions and disciplines that you will need to focus sharply on how to work effectively. Our relative freedom of action, less structured work practices, almost endless range of possible activities to engage in and our loose accountability arrangements, all these are strengths only if we have effective ways of working individually and corporately.

## How to be effective

How to know what to do and how to be effective in doing it are key issues for all of us and particularly in the more unstructured contexts that clergy often face. Behind the question 'what do I do?' lie the deep issues of vocation, discernment of the work of the Holy Spirit and the co-operation of the Church in that work. But seeking to be conscious and aware of what you are doing with your time and why will always be important. It is a stewardship matter that, whether we are by nature relaxed or driven, we need to address. To step back on a regular basis and to take a look at the way we are using broad chunks of our day is an essential discipline that can help us to avoid simply responding to the next request or event. Being clear about what you are doing with your time is the step which leads to knowing how much of what you are doing is related to your own or others' purposes. You can then move on to consider whether you are doing it as effectively as possible.

There are a variety of techniques available to help in assessing how our time is being used and perhaps the simplest is to make conscious use of your diary not just as a record of appointments, but as a key administrative tool. Start, for example, by making a list of the different general ways in which time is used over a typical week: administration, pastoral, liturgical, project activities. Then without any detailed analysis, make an estimate of how you think you use your time. In the following week ensure that you keep a reasonably detailed record in your diary of what you are doing through the week, and at the end of the following week, without having tried to change your normal work pattern, analyse your diary into the listed categories. Compare the results with your original estimates and prepare to be surprised at the differences between reality and perception. It can be a helpful starting point for reassessing ways of working.

When you know how you are spending your time, you can begin to look again at what you actually want to spend it on and set about devising systems to bring about the balance that is right for your particular personality, gifts and context.

## Administration – ministering to ministry

The word 'administration' speaks of there being something important about ministry in the administrative task although for most parish clergy administration is unlikely in itself to be at the heart of their ministry. But it needs to be done and done efficiently if the core tasks of ministry are to be given space to flourish and to be done well. Indeed administration might be thought of as the work of ministering to your ministry.

The key to administration is system – the ability to discern clearly the different subsections of the total task and to devise regular patterns and routines to enable them to be undertaken in a timely and effective manner. It is these regular patterns and routines which make up the ministry that enable the different ministerial tasks to be undertaken effectively.

There are sections of the total ministerial task that are likely to be common to all parochial clergy: the preparation of liturgy in all its many forms, the development of mission – the occasional offices, the provision of means of communication, the pastoral task, the management and maintenance of buildings and the teaching ministry in all its various manifestations, among many others. In addition each parish will have its own particular tasks according to its circumstances, perhaps involving the development of new structures for the church: cell church, team ministry, new forms of partnership and collaboration. It is quite likely that there will be a significant development initiative, perhaps for the better use of the church buildings or for new forms of outreach in partnership with groups in the local community.

Each of these individual tasks needs to be identified and 'mapped' so that a clear picture of the total task in hand can be generated. Whether at the start of a new ministry or at regular intervals as time in a parish progresses, it is worth taking time to stand back and consider the different areas of ministry that make up the total ministerial task. It is when these different areas are clearly mapped as part of a total picture that the administrative task becomes clearer, both in its total size and in its relationship to the different pieces of work. If you are reasonably proficient at the keyboard and screen – and this will increasingly be essential – then what is known as 'mind mapping' software can be very helpful. Mind maps are a way of setting out visually the full range of our activities and very helpfully the interconnections between them.

## Resourcing administration

It is at this point that it can all become rather daunting since clarity about task often highlights just how much administration there is to be done. The resourcing question then needs to be seriously addressed, initially with close colleagues such as churchwardens, but at some point with the PCC. The resources that may need to be brought to bear will depend on the situation, including your particular gifts and inclinations and those of your colleagues in the church. There is nothing heroic in insisting on undertaking the administrative ministry alone and the questions that always arise about where the money for the new equipment is to come from, about the office space or the salary of an administrator, will need to be addressed head on. It is not sufficient to allow the 'we can't afford it' response to dominate a careful discussion about where the parish's priorities lie and how the church really wishes its minister to use his or her time.

But in addition to these practical points, administration in the hands of the vicar can so easily compound the problem to which our Church of England parish culture is prone – the tendency to centralize every task on the minister. The holding of all records on the vicar's computer, the arranging of all meetings and their agendas by the vicar and the keeping of all files in the vicar's study, all these can lead to real difficulties, including problems of continuity between one vicar and the next. Perhaps even more importantly, such arrangements speak of control, power and the absence of a genuinely corporate approach to the life of the church.

It is for these kinds of reasons that parish offices and parish administrators are important, both as being likely to lead to more effective administration, but also because they represent an approach that encourages collaborative ministries. For you as vicar to have a personal secretary is not at all the same thing as having a parish secretary or administrator, and is more likely to be part of centralizing work around yourself and a consequent deskilling of others, than to lead to an appropriate and effective administrative ministry in the parish.

For most churches it will make for a far more effective use of clergy to have a part- or even full-time administrator or parish secretary and for smaller parishes this will often be achievable in partnership with neighbours. Clergy time used on administration cannot be used on something else and most parishes, if they consider it openly, would prefer your time to be used on the 'something else'.

Of course this is not to say that it is just a matter of handing the administration over to someone else. There is much that you can do individually to equip or re-equip yourself for administrative ministry and certainly recourse to an administrator should not be seen as simply a substitute for a needed change in attitude or skills by the parish priest. In the end, you will need to remain responsible for the total ministerial task and how it is to be well served.

At any point in our ministry it is worth stopping to consider what new skills are needed. Would additional technology assist in the task and how would I learn about the effective use of PC or laptop, Powerpoint, Publisher or Excel, email or the range of other modern technologies that have become the foundation of effective administration in recent years? What time-management or other management training courses are available? The means of learning the effective application of these skills is usually easily available in local colleges or sometimes through courses provided by the diocese.

Tools such as these are there to be used but they are not substitutes for the necessary work of devising appropriate processes to provide the frameworks within which they can be used effectively. Use of email, for example, can become a burden unless you have thought through your attitude to it. Is an email to be treated as a letter or as a telephone call? What should be saved and can it be retrieved at will? What communications are appropriate to email rather than a telephone call or a face-to-face meeting? How you deal with these kinds of questions will influence the style of your ministry and how you are perceived in the church and community. Someone who closets themselves in their study with the PC will raise as many eyebrows as the person who doesn't reply to letters, phone calls or emails and who lets paper simply pile up.

## Attitude to administration

To be reasonably proficient in the technologies is one thing, but underlying these remains the unchanging need to have an attitude that leads to the administrative task being undertaken systematically and in a regular and timely manner. Does the structure of your day include a specific time when the post – letters and emails – is opened and responded to? What is your filing system like and does it facilitate administration? How is the meetings schedule arrived at? Too often it can be much more a case of just accepting each need as it comes along, than as part of a more or less deliberate patterning of the day or the week. It is process that holds tasks together in a patterned manner and that leads to a more effective ministry. In many aspects of life we have learned how to follow effective processes as part of growing up into adulthood: we know that a conversation should follow some reasonably logical steps; that preparing a meal effectively requires a series of tasks to be undertaken in a structured sequence. So it is with our work. In the relatively unstructured world of work that clergy are usually placed in, with demands upon time arriving from many sources and an apparently high degree of freedom to accept or refuse, devising appropriate processes can fall by the wayside. Our pattern of life can then become essentially responsive with the urgent driving out the important and the separation of different areas of ministry from one another becoming more difficult with all the consequences for effectiveness that follow.

---

**Work process: using 'to do' lists**

You can't get much more basic than this, but nor can you do without a regular time – perhaps daily – to review what is currently outstanding. Even mobile phones now have a 'to do' facility in the menu.

There's no substitute for keeping a running list that has your main current activities as headings and a subsidiary list of things you have to do under each. How satisfying it is to be able physically to cross them off. I have even been known to add an item that I have just completed just to have the satisfaction of crossing it off.

This task can be a prayerful time as well, an opportunity to offer individuals, challenges and situations to God, and when the list seems too great, to seek to hand the sense of burden over.

---

**Work process: patterns to the day and the week**

Allocating blocks of time regularly through the day or week to particular types of task can be helpful. Time to review the week ahead with colleagues at the start of the week may seem obvious, but the obvious is not always done. Time at the beginning of the day or some days with your parish secretary or administrator to deal with current tasks; blocks of time over a month to meet with churchwardens, team leaders or other key people. Knowing your temperament will help: some work better to deadlines, others need to be ready well in advance. Whichever it is, be clear about the tasks ahead and allocate time to their preparation. Don't be 'ambushed' by your diary – have a seven-day page spread rather than a page per day diary.

# Administration and management

If, as I have previously suggested, administration is thought of as ministering to ministry, then it is probably not at the heart of the parish priest's task and therefore belongs in someone else's hands, someone who is particularly called to that ministry.

Even if administration is not one of the core ministries for you or for clergy generally, management on the other hand almost certainly is or should be. That is not a statement that many clergy wish to hear or would willingly accept, largely because 'management' and 'manager' have become words with negative connotations to many across a range of professions – the hospital manager, the practice manager, government managers. A manager is easily portrayed as an undesirable 'middleman' between those who do the real work with people – patients, pupils or parishioners – and the leaders and directors who set the policies and directions. Managers are then at best a perhaps necessary evil, but are more creatures of the system than part of the delivery team. But it is certainly just as possible to argue a different understanding and one which is based in the Ordinal's description of priests as called to be 'messengers, watchmen, and stewards of the Lord'. That is also quite a good description of a manager. Parish clergy as managers are both called to be responsible under God for 'watching over' and discerning the overall context and needs of the church and the local community. Both are called to be the 'messenger' who brings and holds together in mutuality the range of people whom they serve. As 'stewards' you are called to lead people in the church and in partnership with the church, into the most effective use of the resources – people and their gifts, property, money and much else – that God has provided. This is what it is to be a manager and it is in fact not so different in practice from the traditional role that the incumbent has always held in the local church. Presidency at the Eucharist, chairing of the PCC and, jointly with the bishop, responsibility for the cure of souls, over the centuries have *de facto* placed upon the clergy the responsibility for managing, for stewarding the life of the local church.

Of course, the emphasis is now rightly much more on collaborative ministry, on collective action and on partnership than in the past, including particularly an emphasis on the complementary ministries of others, lay and ordained, in the local church or churches. But if anything this increases the 'managerial' role of the clergy as one who presides, shepherds and stewards across the increasingly wide range of people and activities that make up the mission and ministry of the local church. To this should be added a reaffirmation and probably a strengthening of the representative role to the wider local community as we turn away from acquiescence in the privatized place allocated to the church in recent decades.

As we move towards recognizing and accepting a wider variety of gifts in the life of the church and the wider variety of ministries that are authorized and affirmed, the managerial task becomes more complex and requires careful and skilful work with people as individuals and in the variety of teams and groups through which their ministries are exercised. The first skill of course is self-restraint, how to hold back from doing it yourself, however much you may believe that you would do it better. The balanced composition of groups and committees becomes of increasing importance. Terms of reference, job descriptions and patterns of review become essential instruments.

All of this means paying particularly careful attention to the formal structures of the church's life and in particular to the PCC. You must have a PCC and you should normally chair it; it will have to have the required ex officio membership and few things lead more quickly to trouble than a perception that the representational rules are being ignored or bent. But that still leaves plenty of room for agreement on the most effective ways of managing the life of the church. The key is clarity about who does what, how in the end decisions are taken, and a firm understanding that in the end in our system, all is underpinned by the rule of law.

## Management and leadership

Management and leadership are rightly distinguished in most contemporary business texts, but for parish clergy significant elements of each are likely to be quite closely held in the same person. The vicar will continue to be the head of the leadership team, the chief steward or manager and the person accountable for the administration of the resources of the church. This is not a return to a singular model of leadership and perhaps we can draw by analogy on other professions, seeing in ourselves something of the senior partner in the medical or legal practice, the headteacher in the school or the managing director of the company. Each of these operates within a corporate team, but each has a distinctive set of responsibilities. Of course, clergy are not precisely any one of these things because the church is not a medical practice, school or business; it is a church – something different, but not so different that there is nothing to compare with, borrow from and give to.

## Awareness of the wider parish

For all that the concept of parish is changing and new forms of clustering and collaboration are rightly being encouraged, and for all that network, cell, community and virtual churches are growing, nevertheless place, locality and neighbourhood remain fundamental to most people's experience of life. The parish system, however it evolves and is supplemented by other approaches to mission and ministry, remains the normal context for most clergy.

If you are to be effective in leadership, management and administration, then building into the yearly round regular ways of assessment and review is essential. Contexts do change rapidly and a few years can see substantial changes in the ethnicity or faith of significant groups, wholesale new housing developments, major regeneration schemes and much more that will change the picture dramatically. What that means is that there continues to be the need to build into the normal round a variety of regular means of checking that the local church collectively still has a common and real picture of itself and its activities and of its wider parish community.

There are some opportunities built in to the system but others may need to be developed. The Annual Parochial Church Meeting (APCM) is one regular yearly opportunity. An annual away day for the PCC or wider church for reflection is, of course, another and there are many possible variations on the theme of churches taking time away to look at themselves more reflectively.

Where there have been significant changes and developments in the wider community, or of course where some new development in the life of the church itself is proposed, it may well be important to undertake a parish audit or survey for which there are many ready-made models available. The Shaftesbury Society,[1] for example, offers a helpful set of resources built around a 'prayer, action, reflection' cycle which has been developed in partnership with many churches, and there are many other helpful resources of this kind. Indeed formal or informal surveys can become a regular feature paralleling in a small way the practice of the local supermarket – few people have a better picture of the composition, lifestyle and location of the local population than the supermarket manager because it is essential to their continued existence that they know and respond to their local community not once but on a continuing basis.

How to do the APCM is a perennial question. Legally and practically, there has to be one for the presenting of reports, the adoption of the electoral roll and the electing of people to PCC and various committees or Synod, but the approach is often more about how to minimize the occasion than about how it could be put to use to look at some of the bigger picture questions. The trouble, of course, is that to do it differently and on more than a minimalist basis can be very time consuming in terms of preparation and notoriously the attendance can be rather modest. But the APCM presents a real opportunity to attend to the bigger picture. The key elements are that the big picture questions should genuinely capture something that is felt by the congregation to be significant, that they should be well prepared and presented – not someone just standing out in front and reading out a report – and that they lead on to some development in the life of the church. In addition, where churches offer hospitality to local community groups or are in partnership with them, they should be fully included in the Annual Meeting and will often bring some new perspectives to bear on what are sometimes thought to be internal church issues. The task of setting the bigger picture does not of course fall solely to you as vicar. Building up the picture is the shared task of the local church as a whole, undertaken formally and informally by groups and individuals who after all live and work as part of the wider community. But however you gain it, unless you have a clear if broad picture of your context in mind, you will not have the groundwork for effective leadership and management in the church. The gathering of the big picture has real value in its own right but it is also the basis for clarifying the vision and purposes of the church.

## Being selective and purposeful

It is often said that we have information overload, and who has not grumbled about what seems to be an ever increasing and often unasked for river of papers, emails or questionnaires from a variety of sources? More information – the bigger picture – is all very well but it is not always easy to decide how to shape and pattern it, how to isolate and then bin or delete what is trivia or not relevant. Just as on some front doors there is the notice 'no circulars or unsolicited mail', so it is not uncommon for clergy to adopt an attitude of wholesale rejection towards one or other category of information – 'I never read those.' But this is not quite right and runs the risk of descending into a 'safe mode' which isolates from the wider common experiences and of course risks opportunities being missed.

One approach to these issues is derived from Stephen Covey's *Seven habits of highly effective people*.[2] His third habit uses four categories in a 'time management matrix': urgent/not urgent and important/not important. Information in the form of paper, emails or telephone calls can be assessed, often intuitively, into four categories: the important and urgent, the not urgent but important, the urgent but not important and those that are neither urgent nor important. Covey commends the second group as the one on which to spend most time – the first is essentially about crisis management and the latter two about trivia.

Whether the language of mission statements and action plans is used or not, what is essential is that a church corporately has some real understanding, not only of where it currently is, but also of where it would like to head for and how it is going to get there.

## Agreeing the process

This is the essential work of setting priorities and of choosing one course rather than another. Are the church buildings fit for their purpose? Is the pattern and timing of worship right? Are the governance arrangements of the church best suited to the present stage in the life of the church? To come to conclusions about such issues as a church requires careful attention to process if they are not simply to be imposed or manipulated. It is never easy, involving in all probability significant change and the shifts of power and influence that often accompany change.

Careful work on process can often make a real contribution to achieving a common set of purposes and plans, whether for a major change in the structures of the church, in the work towards a major buildings reordering project or some new approach to mission. By process I mean here an agreed set of steps which, if pursued, will lead to corporate decisions on the matters in question. A process needs to include all the significant steps that must be taken. It must set out who is to be involved and in what ways; it should specify how decisions are to be taken at each stage and by whom; and it should include a clear timetable. Commitment to an agreed process by all parties will not avoid the need for tough discussion and sometimes painful decisions, but it will do much to minimize confusion, sidetracking and prevarication. Putting forward a proposal for an agreed process may bring into the open people and issues that might otherwise lie hidden and may at the outset lead to agreement on how they are to be resolved. In general, the more a process involves only the people of the church making their own decisions and the less it has recourse to outside arbiters, the better. External reference, however well intentioned or impartial, will rarely satisfy and may only store up resentment. There may of course be some limited cases where the legal frameworks may require an external arbiter and this will be the case, for example, with decisions by the Chancellor to grant or withhold a faculty.

## The people

It would be good to be able to say that the church shows the world an excellent model of how the people with whom it engages should be treated – as angels entertained unawares, as Christ in the other, as neighbours loved as ourselves. But this is not always so and there are as many examples of the best in secular organizations as there are in the Church. The relationship between, for example, diocesan structures and individuals is a complex and messy mix of history, custom and practice, legislative provision, private patronage, and prejudice and the experience for many clergy has by no means always been a good one.

But whether it is in relation to employed people, volunteers, parishioners or anyone else you need to strive to pay attention to the ways that in practice you relate to others. This will mean engaging effectively with the details of employment legislation and codes of good practice for the people you employ (and indeed some areas such as disability, health and safety and child protection are matters of law that must be complied with); it may well mean contracts and letters of agreement for volunteers; it will certainly mean being fully aware of best practice in pastoral situations. On the one hand you need to be fully aware of professional standards and on the other you need to retain your humanity and avoid falling into a correct and cold protective legalism. As required of us in the bishop's charge in the Ordinal, you must set the Good Shepherd always before you as your pattern.

There are some rules of thumb to keep in mind in all this, and perhaps the most important is to be clear with people. For employment, clear and agreed job descriptions, reporting and review arrangements, letters of contract, terms and conditions are all essential; for volunteers – from churchwardens to flower arrangers – clarity about expectations, roles, reviews and especially about endings are all best expressed in a written form after discussion. There is no shortage of models available for all these things and wheels do not have to be reinvented.

All this does not have to be bureaucratic or administratively burdensome, but clarity of these kinds does demonstrate a concern for the other person, that they have been attended to and their offering taken seriously.

A further rule of thumb: encourage the widest participation, want to say 'yes' to people's hopes and aspirations for involvement, nurture the least offering and 'let a thousand flowers bloom'. We are after all members of the Body of Christ each with our own important part to play in the whole and it is when there is a sense of openness and encouragement to participate that a community begins to flourish and to discover that it contains all the gifts it needs to be the whole church locally.

## Making the plans

You may see the big picture, be clear about your purpose and have excellent processes in position, but without detailed plans that speak about who is going to do what, when they will do it and where, nothing lasting will be accomplished. This is where an understanding of incarnation begins to bite because the created order is all about the way in which a multitude of small activities and events come together to create the dynamic and changing world which God loves so much. This is about attention to the detail of finding resources, to the legal frameworks, the committees and the many other practicalities that must be attended to.

Increasingly, churches are stepping out into partnerships with other organizations in the wider community as part of their plans for ministry for mission. This may involve the sharing of part of the church building, issues of appropriate uses, loss of direct control, the handling of substantial sums of money and contractual relationships with public sector bodies, all of which may be new experiences for the church. So often the core tasks fall to the vicar, either because they have been the vicar's initiative or because 'there is no one else to do it', frequently despite an absence of any relevant training or experience. These partnerships are, I believe, an important aspect of the future mission of the Church, but you do need to have your eyes wide open to the substantial pressures to which they can lead. It is important to take careful and early advice from within the diocese – from archdeacon, registrar, resourcing advisers and others and if at all possible from specialist consultants.

In making these or other plans in pursuit of our purposes and priorities, our institutional context has some very particular aspects which need to be carefully navigated. The Church of England is something of a chameleon which takes on distinctively different appearances from different perspectives. It can sometimes appear to be a corporate institution much like any other, with corporate governance, strategic planning processes, human resources managers and all the rest. From other perspectives it can seem to be much more like a federation of independent dioceses, or indeed of parishes within any diocese. And from another view it can appear to be constructed as a representative democracy with its three-tiered parliamentary style synods. It is of course some of these things and none of them, and this means that in constructing our plans it is important to be realistic and clear about the institutional context within which you are working. It may be even more important to ensure that any partners you are working with, particularly where they are unfamiliar with the Church and its ways, are not misled, albeit unintentionally. What degrees of freedom do you have to work within in relation to buildings, for example? What levels of financial support or technical expertise can you reliably call upon from the diocese or wider Church? In what matters does the authority to take decisions rest with the local church or elsewhere?

Mistaken assumptions about these things can lead to real problems later on when courses of action can be quite difficult to reverse. In general local churches have more freedom to be innovative and enterprising than is commonly assumed and bishops, archdeacons and diocesan secretaries have less power to restrict and limit than is often thought. What is important is that plans be clearly located within a worked-through framework of picture, purpose and process and backed by a shared commitment within the church to take them forward. There is everything to be said for encouraging the development of new and enterprising ways of living out and sharing the gospel even where these do not fit easily with the established patterns and structures of the wider Church context.

It is not always clearly understood by people within the Church, let alone beyond it, that because the Church of England remains (at least for the time being) the established church, it operates under Parliamentary legislative provisions, albeit largely delegated through the General Synod, and this does provide a particular framework within which local churches must live and work and have their being. *The Pastoral Measure, The Faculty Jurisdiction Measure* and *The Church Representation Rules,* among others, will have a significant impact on many aspects of what we seek to undertake in the local church particularly where buildings are concerned. These are not the constructs of the Church alone, but have the full force of law and so observance is not just a matter of obedience or otherwise, but of enforceable legislation.

Faculties are often felt to be the bane of local churches seeking to adapt their buildings to present-day needs even in the most modest ways, and it is the case that much will depend upon the attitudes of members of the Diocesan Advisory Committees (DAC) and the Chancellors, the Amenity Societies and their representatives and the archdeacon, not to mention members of the congregation and wider community. Where there is a genuine desire by all concerned to enable significant changes to be made, albeit through a careful process which is intended to benefit the mission of the local church in its community, then all can be happily, if usually lengthily, achieved. But this is too often not the case and frustration, delay and additional cost can be the result – to the detriment of the Church's mission.

In all cases careful preparation with an architect, working from an early stage with the archdeacon and DAC, early drafting of Statements of Significance and Need, will all pay dividends. The use of Temporary Reordering Certificates (TRC) under the Care of Churches and Ecclesiastical Jurisdiction Measure 1990 is not as widely known as might be expected and, on the authority of the archdeacon, very helpfully permits a 12-month period of experimentation. This can enable quite significant changes to be experienced physically in a way that is not possible from architects' sketches and congregations' imaginations, while providing security for those who are reluctant to agree to a definite decision. The TRC requires that at the end of the period, a faculty must be applied for or everything put back to the way it was before. In some dioceses the 'de minimis' provisions have been revisited to enable less restrictive interpretations of what requires a faculty and it is to be hoped that all DACs will keep this under review.

If in the end none of this is fruitful then, where a PCC is clear that their project is necessary to the mission of the church, they should take their courage in their hands. If the issue is with the DAC, then it is quite possible to appeal direct to the Chancellor, an approach which was successful in one case in Birmingham Diocese. Where the difficulty lies with an Amenity Society, it is well to remember that they have no veto and that it is the Chancellor who grants a faculty. The Chancellor will be aware that the opening sections of the Measure make it clear that the mission needs of the local church – 'pastoral necessity' – must be at the heart of the decision and it is encouraging to note that Chancellors have increasingly widely interpreted what may be permitted within a church building under faculty. Amenity Societies – and indeed others – may now be required to pay Consistory Court costs if they are considered by the Chancellor to have acted unreasonably and PCCs should not easily be dissuaded from their plans by the threat of proceedings in the Consistory Court, alarming though the prospect can sound at first.

*The Pastoral Measure*, currently under revision, is the other substantial legislative provision which can bear on plans that parishes or groups of parishes may have for collaborative ventures or for the redundancy of their buildings to enable them to be used for other purposes. In general one may say that Schemes under the Measure proceed only very slowly, partly because of the extended rights of representation that are given to all parties. Where possible it is best to seek creative solutions that do not require formal approval under *The Pastoral Measure*, for example, developing the idea of covenant, not binding in law, but deeply binding in our understanding of the relationship between God and ourselves.

God will continue to call, and the church will continue to accept for ordained ministry, men and women with the widest variety of gifts, personality and experience. Not all will be gifted in administration, management or leadership and we should certainly not give the impression that these are the greatest gifts. But they are important and should be cultivated and nurtured if we are to steward to the best of our abilities all that has been given.

# 8

# Leadership and teamwork

Chris Edmondson

## What is a team?

The word leadership is derived in English from an old North European word meaning a path, roadway or course of a ship at sea. It is a journey or movement word. Likewise, 'team' is also a dynamic word. In early English usage it often referred to groups of animals united together with the aim of moving something from one point to another driven by a 'teamster'. Apparently when geese fly south for winter, the V formation they adopt is not just to impress any onlookers. By flying in this formation, owing to the aerodynamics involved, the whole flock gains 71 per cent more flying range than if each bird flew alone. They enable each other to create a synergy in which each one is able to accomplish more as a result of being linked up with the rest of the flock. Over time, in the English language, the word 'team' came to mean any example of people coming together and working for some common purpose, as in a sports team. The word team therefore describes an event in which two or more people covenant together to live out some sense of mutual purpose.

It is my conviction that if the Church in England is going to recover its nerve, and rediscover its calling in the twenty-first century, it will be by means of people with a vision and understanding of being team leaders and team builders. Learning to be team players and leading by example are the means that will enable this synergy. I would go as far as to say that nothing in the contemporary church should be done by any individual alone, but everyone should be part of some kind of identifiable team to which they are accountable, and from which they can also receive support.

## Categories of team

Teams have different aspects some of which are more dominant than others. I find it helpful to identify three categories of team. First, there are teams that can be described as 'generative'. Such teams operate out of a well-defined, mutually accepted leadership, with a clear sense of purpose and vision. Constant reminders are given as to why the team exists, and each member of the team is using their God-given gifts and growing to their full potential. Synergy is being experienced, others observe the attractiveness and effectiveness of the team and, as a result of the team's relationships and work, other teams are spawned from it. Discussion and debate in a generative team is open and, although sometimes vigorous, 'hidden agendas' have no place in its life. When there is conflict, it is creative, and the resultant outcomes are to everyone's benefit.

Another style of team, which is found all too often in church life, is the 'habitual' team. This kind of team may once have had a clear sense of purpose and vision, but for various reasons this has been lost along the way. It exists because it exists – 'as it was in the beginning, is now and evermore shall be'. It is there simply as a part of church life. Another example of this kind of team can be seen in a group which is obliged by Church law to exist, but is somehow unable to function above that level of obligation. This can be how a church council or equivalent group ends up operating. It meets, does its work, more or less efficiently depending on the style of leadership and the personalities in the group, but there is little or no passion or enthusiasm for the task, and it fails to fulfil its potential. The effect on its members is frustrating and draining rather than energizing, and when conflict occurs, which it does frequently, it is usually over secondary, not to say trivial, matters.

The third and potentially most destructive team is the 'toxic' team. Here there is usually no overall sense of vision and purpose, and the dominant feature is 'me first': my way at all costs. Not surprisingly, morale is low and conflict predominates with little or no capacity to bring resolution. Such teams tend to be very territorial and defensive in their role, and are a danger to the church or organization of which they are a part.

It is possible for the habitual and even the toxic team to start to function more effectively, given the right leadership and probably some changes in team membership, but the prognosis for some groups is frankly terminal, and they need to be allowed to die. From a leadership point of view, this can be very challenging and costly, but my experience tells me that if things are allowed to drift, the situation will only worsen and have a poisonous effect on the whole life and ministry of a church. It is helpful to bear these three categories in mind, and to use them as a filter through which to assess the health and effectiveness of whatever teams you find are in place, especially when coming new into a situation.

## Stages of team development

There are four commonly recognized stages of team development, described in these terms: forming, storming, norming and performing.

*Forming:* When the group or team first forms, it has no established way of working. The members are like hesitant swimmers, dipping their toes in the water. There is a lot of uncertainty around, and as a result, people will be unsure how to tackle the task, and possibly how to relate to one another. Relationships at this stage inevitably tend to be rather superficial. Some individuals may begin to assert themselves and one or two may try to take advantage of the new situation to impose their ideas, especially if they have felt frustrated in the past. So, if your predecessor was essentially authoritative, and you want to bring a much more collaborative style of leadership into the situation, people in the church will need time to understand and learn to trust the new approach. Your expectations might be clear as to how the church council could (and should) operate, but those with whom you are working will need some time to 'acclimatize'.

As people realize what the new approach might involve, there may then be some clashes of expectations; this is known as the *storming* stage. This may lead to some panic, on the part of the leader and the team, like non-swimmers being expected to jump in at the deep end. Such a period can be a testing time for all concerned, when disagreements surface and conflicts appear, as the particular team or group tries to sort itself out. In order to promote an atmosphere of peace and harmony, it can be tempting as a leader to contain or suppress such emotions. This is actually not a good thing, because behavioural norms and group/team character are beginning to evolve, and if hidden agendas are kept hidden or grievances secretly nursed, the effectiveness of the team will be limited in the longer term. This 'storming' stage is when you know the 'honeymoon' is over and the real work of team building has begun. It should be noted that some groups of people never get beyond this stage. However, if you keep your nerve and realize that it is not the end of the process, as people get used to working together, stop struggling and start to help each other stay afloat, then the *norming* phase has been reached. This represents a stage where there is more of a sense of trust between people, more cohesion, acceptance and ownership of the challenges and problems being faced and a recognition of each other's strengths and gifts. This is the stage when consensus is reached, perhaps initially simply about how the group ought to work. Agreement over the way decisions are taken usually takes longer to achieve since this is based on shared values. One danger to be watched at this stage is that, in reaction to the relative chaos of the first two stages, with some sense of relief, people start to find security in formal procedures and systems. The 'generative' slips into the 'habitual'.

*Performing* is when the team has reached a stage of true acceptance and indeed delight in working together. People feel more at ease with one another, are clear about the purpose of the team, the particular part each one can play, and the gifts that each can bring to the whole. The move from 'norming' to 'performing' is frequently marked by the replacement of formal systems by strong informal relationships. The team is becoming a generative one with the values and characteristics outlined above. Or to continue the swimming metaphor, the team is now ready for synchronized swimming!

It is important to realize that if membership of the team changes, or if the team encounters major problems, then it may need to go through the cycle again. Part of the leader's task is to help the team address issues that might arise at each stage. Simply because conflict has been faced and dealt with in the past, it does not mean that it will not recur in the future.

Whether in a clergy team, a local church leadership team or a church council, understanding these stages and what is going on above and beneath the surface can make an enormous difference, both to the achievement of the church's vision and the development of individuals within the team.

## Knowing your team

Another insight which I have found helpful, especially in the early stages of a new ministry, or when team membership changes, is the well-known study on management by Dr R. Meredith Belbin, formerly of the Industrial Training Unit in Cambridge. He undertook some research to try to answer two questions: why are some management teams more successful than others, and what makes for a successful team? For the research, the Administrative Staff College at Henley was used as a laboratory over a seven-year period. The results, first published in 1981, have made a very significant contribution to understanding how teams function, and how they can work more effectively. From my own experience of making use of this tool, and talking with others who have used it, the insights it reveals have much wider application than simply to secular management teams.

From the research, Belbin identified that it was possible to predict which teams would work well over time, by using personality tests to examine the mixture of personalities and gifts in the team. The essence of the research revealed that in effective teams, people contribute in two dimensions – through their functional role (their task within the team), and in their team role (style of interacting with others). Both are important, and, for a team to work well, it is necessary to have the right people in each functional role, as well as to identify their team roles.[1]

This Henley research identified two types of successful team. The first is the classic balanced team in which all the roles are filled, and the truth is that most of us will neither inherit nor be able easily to put in place such a team. But I would suggest that the second option is more attainable. Here the team is, or has the potential to become, a group of people committed to being in that team, more self-aware in regard to their style of interacting with others, and clearer about their role in the team tasks.

This is only one way of looking at things but, particularly in a new situation, it can be very helpful in raising people's self-awareness, and seeing whether the different personalities in the team are operating out of their strengths and gifts. Once this approach is understood and the people involved have completed the questionnaire,[2] you are in a better position to assess whether the team fits the successful team stereotypes. Coming at it another way, your team members may already be clear about task definitions and functions within the team but it may also be helpful to discuss the roles that people fulfil within the team. Are you making the best use of the individual gifts and personalities of the team members? Is everyone functioning at their best (bearing in mind that some people can manage several roles whereas others need more of a single focus)?

## Types of team in the local church

### The core leadership team

The first type might be called a 'leadership team' whose main task under God is to see the 'big picture' and to seek a sense of purpose and direction for the future. This will involve developing strategy, clarifying values, identifying key opportunities to be pursued, appointing people to key positions, whether paid or as volunteers, and maintaining contact with other churches and other agencies in the area. In my last parish, such tasks were carried out by what we called the 'staff team'. This consisted of the vicar, curate, youth and children's worker, community worker (all paid posts) and the two churchwardens. We met on a weekly basis. The first hour of each meeting was a mixture of Bible study, prayer and some sharing of what was going on for each of us in our lives. After that, we sought to attend to the 'oversight' tasks as outlined above, together with any pressing concerns for the church. Three times a year we held an away day, when there was more time to revisit the vision to which we were working, and to think through possible new developments. We were very clear not to usurp what was rightly the role of the church council, so would bring recommendations which they could then discuss and come to a decision about. Clear and open communication between a 'leadership' group and the church council is vital if misunderstandings are not to occur. Another way of applying the same principle might be to use the PCC standing committee, or, in a multi-parish benefice, to call the churchwardens together as the basis of such a team. However this principle is worked out in each locality, I am convinced that a core leadership team, who can think strategically and encourage risk-taking, is vital for the health and growth of a church.

## The church council

A second type of team in Church of England terms would be the church council. In other denominations, the equivalent group might be the deacons or elders. Here there are some prescribed tasks laid down in Canon Law, which have at their heart the call to 'co-operate with the incumbent in the ministry and mission of the Church'. All too often, however, the bar is set too low, and so these statutory bodies do not operate in a 'generative' way. Having worked in four very different local church contexts, from the deeply rural to inner urban and suburban, it is my conviction and experience that this particular team has much more potential than is often realized. It may take time to see this fulfilled, but I believe this should be our aim as leaders (see Chapter 5 above).

Out of one such PCC day, came a new method of working that began to make their regular meetings both more effective and enjoyable. Three priorities were agreed for the forthcoming year, with different members of the church council opting to focus on one of them, creating three sub-groups for that period. For the next few months, following an initial period of devotions together, members divided up into the three groups for about 45 minutes, and then came back to share their discussions and progress with the rest of the church council. After that they dealt with the statutory business and other necessary agenda items. This enabled people to use their best energies early on in the meeting in an area about which they felt some passion and/or had some expertise, and increased the sense of 'ownership' about the work of the church council as a whole.

## Task teams

In church life, other teams are made up of people who fulfil various specialist functions. These might include a group of children's or youth work leaders, a group committed to maintain the church plant, an intercessory prayer group, house/cell group leaders, a healing prayer team, an outreach visiting team, those involved in music and drama in worship, flower arrangers – the list is endless! It is likely that if these teams exist already, some will be working better than others. Hopefully some of the earlier material in this chapter can help in seeing ways to improve things where necessary, or to 'grip' a situation which has been drifting and if all else fails to 'bury' it.

## The minister's key roles

There are three key roles that the minister plays in relation to such teams. One is to affirm and appreciate people who 'get on with the job' and demonstrate a high degree of commitment to the task, which can often go unrecognized or unappreciated. Too many clergy really do take people for granted. The word 'appreciate' means to 'raise in value'. Every time we practise affirmation and appreciation in the team context, we not only encourage the team member personally, but also add value to the team as a whole. The second role is to put in place appropriate support and training for people who are giving of themselves in different areas of ministry and service. This will further their sense of being valued, and help them to continue when they feel discouraged. Thirdly, it is important to ensure the right people are co-ordinating these teams, and that on a regular basis those leaders meet with the vicar or other leadership team member.

---

In two of the parishes in which I have worked I would meet at least three times a year with the home group leaders. There were various reasons for doing this. One was to give them a new vision for their work and remind them why small groups were important in the life of the church. Another was to give them an opportunity to share encouragements and problems, and to think together about areas for study and action. In my last parish, realizing that, with an increasing number of groups, I was unable personally to give sufficient support, I took two steps to remedy this. The first was to appoint a lay person with a passion for small groups as home group co-ordinator, who also helped produce study material. Secondly, I appointed three 'home group pastors', people who would have oversight of five or six groups, attend them occasionally, and give support to their leaders, especially when they were encountering problems.

---

## Project teams

Fourthly, there are what might be called 'project teams'. These are made up of groups brought together for specific purposes and for a particular time period. If a church is embarking on a building project, a group will need to be set up that includes representatives from the church council, but brings in other people from the congregation or even the wider community, with expertise in areas such as the building trade, tone and image, finance, fund-raising and publicity. Similarly, if a church is going to embark on an evangelistic mission, it will be important to include on the planning team a mixture of ages, personalities and spiritual experience, who can in turn enthuse others in the congregation to see they all can play some part in this venture.

## The individual matters

Effective teams maintain a creative tension between fulfilling the vision, team dynamics and the needs of the individual. Clergy and other leaders in the church need a high level of awareness and ongoing training in the skills required to manage this complex process, because none of the three areas exists in isolation from the others. Furthermore, the sense of team is not built by giving attention to all the elements at the same level throughout the life of the team. Recognition of what should take precedence at any given time is crucial in the process. So for example, in the early stages of team building, the leader's role has a higher profile, as the leader invites, recruits and selects people for the team. In recent years I have found that having three 'C's in mind helps at this point – the potential recruit's *character, competence*, and in team terms, what will be the *chemistry* between people on the team as a result of this appointment. Early on too, leaders unconsciously model the values by which the team will operate. What matters in these early stages, is not so much what the first decisions are, but how they are made. If most contributions come from relatively few people, a pattern will be established. If meetings consistently start late, it quickly becomes acceptable for people to arrive late.

### Dealing with individuals

Turning now to consider in more detail the needs of the individual within the team, one of the most difficult scenarios is how to deal with a team member whose poor performance is adversely affecting the team's work. When you inherit a situation like this, what do you do?

It is important to try to understand the underlying cause of a problem such as this. It may be an issue of motivation, and working on that with the individual may be the right approach to sorting things out. It is also necessary to be patient with people, and be willing to risk giving time to a situation. Investing time in people is an important part of the leader's role. Sometimes when it is evident that time and fresh support is not going to make any difference, like Paul and Barnabas in Acts 15, there has to be a 'parting of the ways'. It is then up to the leader to try to help the individual face the fact that being part of the team is, in all honesty, neither working for them nor for the team as a whole. It may be helpful to discuss whether there is another area of church life where the person's gifts can be used more appropriately. This is a very sensitive situation, particularly when the person is a 'volunteer' who may have given many years service in a given area, but facing it square on is sometimes the only answer, and may be the kindest thing to do.

Recognizing that there will always be those individuals who 'underperform' for whatever reason, it is possible as a leader to spend so much time sorting out situations of that kind that the individuals who are working well get neglected, and are not given the support they deserve, or opportunities for further growth and development. Experience shows that in an average congregation, 10 per cent of the people can take up 90 per cent of the minister's time. This proportion is fine, except the problem is that often it is not the right 10 per cent!

# An environment for growth

## Secure but not safe

From the Gospels it is evident that Jesus was a very secure leader to be with, but he could hardly be called safe! This is exemplified in the juxtaposition of phrases like: 'Come to me all whose load is heavy, and I will give you rest' (Matthew 11.28), along with: 'Anyone who wants to come after me must deny themselves, take up their cross and follow me' (Luke 9.23). Jesus, being secure in himself because of his relationship with the Father (John 13.3-5) and because of the way he treated his disciples, created that safe environment in which others were enabled to take risks and thereby grow. Do you make it a priority as a leader to create such an environment?

## Being a conductor, not a soloist

As a musician by background and training, required to be both a soloist and a conductor at different times, I find this a helpful analogy. There is a difference between being independent – which in a team setting can be a sign of insecurity, and fostering interdependence – recognizing our incompleteness without each other, and wanting to see the best in and get the best out of others. As I indicated in the earlier chapter on 'Vision', Nehemiah has in so many ways been an inspiration to me as a model of good leadership. Having been given the vision for rebuilding the walls of Jerusalem, he knew this would be possible only by means of teamwork. His leadership approach was then to inspire the people with the preferred future of a rebuilt rather than ruined Jerusalem, and the task of rebuilding was accomplished by means of individuals being in the right place and using their gifts as part of the whole team. Effective team leadership is not threatened by others' competence, but positively delights in individuals finding themselves in the right places, and thereby excelling and finding fulfilment in what they are doing. Being human, jealousy at others' abilities may have to be fought back at times, but a good team leader is determined that such attitudes will not have the last word.

> **Does anything need to change in your leadership style, in order to fulfil this conductor role; are you willing to give 'solo' parts to others who might perform them better than you do?**

## Ensuring everyone sings from the same song sheet

It is part of the leadership task to enable individuals in a team to agree to and work from the same core values.[3] This is not to stifle vigorous discussion and debate within the team, but is about members being committed to moving in the same overall direction. Another leadership task is to recognize that while individuals need to take personal responsibility for making their relationships work with others on the team, the leader is not free to abdicate where there are personality clashes or major disagreements. If two people are unable to achieve resolution, the leader may have to intervene. My experience is that when handled appropriately, this can be a healing and growing experience for individuals, and the resultant teamwork can be even more effective as a result of working through such issues.

> **What are, or could be the core values that characterize any teams you are called to lead?**

## Risk-taking

It has been said that 'anything that is worth doing does not have to be done perfectly at first'. Individuals on the team need to know that there are built-in risks to being part of such a body, and rather than being fear-bound, encouraged to see this as an exciting challenge. However, from my observation and experience, many leaders and church communities seem to be gripped by such fear. Jesus took great risks as a result of his team selection; the mix of personalities and temperaments was never going to make for an easy ride. But he saw all of them as individuals with potential to grow and develop, even through their failures. So, he could say to Simon Peter: 'Simon, Simon, listen! Satan has demanded to sift all of you like wheat, but I have prayed for you that your faith may not fail; and you, once you have turned back, strengthen your brothers' (Luke 22.31-32).

In the book of Acts, when Peter reported to the church at Jerusalem after the Gentile Pentecost at the house of Cornelius (described in Acts 10), he initially faced considerable hostility and criticism. He had overstepped some precious boundaries by going into a Gentile's house, and eating with uncircumcised people. Yet as he described what had happened, the surprising response of the assembled company was that they praised God saying, 'Then God has given even to the Gentiles the repentance that leads to life' (Acts 11.18). Peter took a huge risk but it was one that literally changed the course of history. How many risks do you take?

## Support and accountability

The seven last words of a dying church could well be: 'We've never done it that way before.' There is no effective leadership that does not include the element of risk whether with individuals, a small team, or a whole church. It means being ready to make or admit mistakes, and to go into uncharted territory. For the leader, along with the emotions of excitement and encouragement will come loneliness and at times heartache. This is why, when we are seeking to lead in the kinds of ways described in this chapter, we ourselves need structures of support and accountability. These might come from 'official' sources, such as an area/rural dean, archdeacon or bishop, and/or through a work consultant or spiritual director.

> **Do you have structures of support and accountability in place? If not, what steps do you need to take to ensure that they are?**

Let Peter Drucker, the American leadership guru, in a lecture on teamwork have the last word:

> **The leader has the task of creating a true whole that is larger than the sum of its parts, a productive entity that turns out to be more than the sum of resources put into it.**

This is both the privilege and challenge of team leadership and good teamwork.

# 9

# Context

## Introduction

David Ison

> The word became flesh and dwelt among us.
>
> (John 1.14)

How long have you been in your current ministerial context? You may still have some boxes left unpacked, or putting up bookshelves may be a distant memory. You may even be thinking about your next move. But however new or old you are in the place where you minister, it is in this context that God is present, for you and for those whom you serve. You may be in a post which has a set time limit, or one in which it feels right that you should stay for about seven years, or even one which is wholly open-ended – it doesn't really matter. In every case, you are called to a presence which is life-long in quality: sharing wholly in this setting now, living in the present moment because it is in the present moment that God is to be found.

## The mission

At the beginning of a new post, a minister comes with his or her own agenda, with its caveats and plans, hopes and fears – and it can feel like being a mole infiltrating an organization in order to change it. The minister may have begun with a clear sense of the God-given task, or may expect it to develop as things go along. But the minister's view of the mission of the church in this new context is not going to be the same as the views of the people already there. The experiences that have formed the minister's vision are different from those that have formed theirs.

## Back to the future

Peter had been a successful team vicar in an outer city suburb. He moved 20 miles to be rector of an inner-city parish with a failing congregation of 15, which had been surviving precariously without a vicar. For his first Christmas there he printed 200 extra service sheets, just as he'd done in his suburban church for the previous seven years. Twenty people turned up. Nothing that he was used to doing persuaded people in the inner-city to come to church. After a year he had a breakdown. With the care and support of a religious community many miles away he began to understand the very different social context in which he was working. He found a couple of students willing to help, started to develop the relationships and faith of the existing elderly church members, and a small number of younger people came to join them. The church developed a ministry with some disadvantaged children and adults in the local community and this eventually transformed its life and worship.

Many churches fear for their future, facing falling numbers and older membership. Their temptation is to look back to when things were more successful and try to regain the past by reasserting tradition: 'We've always done it like this' (which usually means they've forgotten that 'it' changed a few years ago). But this in itself won't work, because the context has moved on. 'Bringing back the Prayer Book' is in itself no more successful in encouraging church growth than 'relevant modern language'. In my experience of working in church settings I've found it helpful to:

- Look back at what worked in the past – being honest, not nostalgic. What was the reality of attendance figures and great achievements, and what has happened since?

- Analyse it – why did we start doing that? What need was it meeting? What were its advantages and weaknesses? What lessons are relevant for the present context?

- And then let go of it – it was good at the time: what does God want us to do now?

There is no going back, but there is building on past experience. What the church did last time might be just the thing this time round as well – or not.

A church in a small rural town had always used the *Book of Common Prayer* for its main weekly service. The parish profile said that they wanted more children and young families to come to church. The new vicar had been inspired by reading a book about how to transform churches, and changed the worship straight away to an informal modern-language *Common Worship* service like the one she'd run during her curacy. Half the choir and some of the members stopped coming, while only a few new people joined. Fortunately the vicar had a cell group meeting after a few weeks, where she talked about the situation and discovered that a friend had done something similar, but had started with a monthly modern service at a different time, and taken some years to grow a different worship pattern. She went home, sat down with the PCC and worked out with them how to meet the needs of existing church members while opening services up to new people. They currently have two morning services of different styles.

Learning from other people's ideas and experience is invaluable. However, it is rarely appropriate simply to transplant a solution from one context into another and expect it to work. The new setting isn't just a different place; the people there have different experiences, gifts and aspirations. They will need to engage with and evaluate the experiences of others before they can discover what will be appropriate for them. The minister needs to take time to work this out with those whom they serve, and not implement her or his ideas as a quick and easy solution to shared problems.

## We too are one

As a minister, you need to listen, and keep on listening, since congregations change and community contexts develop. There will be resources available to help you do that. The church or institution will have done some initial work on their context and what they believe they need. The nearest main library and the Internet will provide reference material (see the National Statistics web site for census results), and through your diocese you may have access to the Geographic Information System for locally-targeted information (see Appendix 2). Ministry and mission support workers in diocese or district, or national mission organizations, can provide audit material for listening to the local community, if the local church hasn't done this recently, and may be able to give guidance on specific issues. I wish I had found out sooner that making use of rural officers, urban co-ordinators, youth workers, social responsibility officers, etc. and their national networks can save a lot of valuable time.

Ministry in context involves improvization and creativity. It isn't like playing a concert where the notes are all written out in advance. It is performance art, where the minister brings particular skills and experience and, together with others, creates something new. Every context has different players, instruments and audience. Old tunes will sound different, and new tunes will have their own distinctive spin. The incarnation of the gospel in any given context won't be quite like it is anywhere else. The (performance) art of ministry requires spending time as a group, and as a church, getting to know one another so that everyone works and plays together.

Relationships are the key to enabling people to feel secure enough to explore visions and possibilities, and to undertake the task of mission. Whatever you do, do it together. Be open to the gifts and insights of everyone, especially those who are on the margins of the church, who may be able to see more clearly than those caught up in it. As St Benedict noted at the beginning of his Rule regarding decision-making in monasteries: 'All are to be called to council, because it is often to the junior person that the Lord reveals what is best.'[1]

## To be a pilgrim

You will also be changed by the context in which you work, and your relationships with the people who are there; so will your family and friends and those who walk alongside you. You travel together with others: be open to grow, even if it seems to threaten your past traditions and ways of doing things. God is in all contexts, and beyond all our parochial traditions: truly seeking him means learning from the experiences of all sisters and brothers in faith, and from those outside the faith community as well.

One of the most uncomfortable aspects of ministry is handling the twin calling to be wholly in a place, and yet at one remove from it. There is a prophetic aspect to ministry which requires the ability to stand back and be distanced, and ask the hard questions – of yourself as well as of others. The ordained minister acts as a link between the local and the universal, within and beyond the church: there will be times when this generates real tensions. But part of the gift the minister brings to a community is being someone with an outsider's perspective: to carry the loneliness of knowing that one day they won't belong there any more.

The next three sections of the book bring this perspective of local and prophetic engagement to bear on particular ministerial contexts. Darren Smith writes out of considerable engagement in urban ministry, with its needs and challenges – for his cat as well as for himself; Jennifer Zarek reflects on the problems and possibilities faced by ministers working in the countryside; Roger Morris focuses on ways of working in larger groups of parishes. There are common themes, in particular the question of limited resources, and all three address issues which they have wrestled with as local ministers. Whatever your own ministerial situation has in common with theirs, there is much to be learned from engaging with the reality of their experience.

For them and for you, this current post is the place where God is to be found – for now. There will be a time to move on and to let go. What others do with it then will be God's business and no longer yours. But until that time comes: 'How awesome is this place! This is none other than the house of God, and this is the gate of heaven.'

# Urban ministry

Darren Smith

## Setting the scene

For nearly two decades now I have ministered on outer city estate parishes in the Midlands. I have worked with a number of other priest colleagues, who have been gifted in many different ways; I have learnt with and from them and, I hope, grown through contact with them. And I have had the joy of working with many hundreds, if not thousands, of ordinary folk for whom these outer estates are home.

I write from within a modern catholic setting. For me, the Eucharist is the centre point from which I find my ministry flows, and to which I believe all ministry tends; it gives a sacrificial context to ministry. In a sense I take for granted the daily round of Offices and Sacraments as the task of the priest. I also take for granted the role of the ordained person as 'parish priest', that we find our meaning and role in the local community in which the church is set.

I recognize, of course, that others come from a different stable with divergent views about the sacramental life of the church, but whatever our background it is important to recognize who we are, where we come from, and what we stand for. Without this basic self-understanding, our ministry becomes simply responsive and in a way less authentic.

In what follows, I want to touch on a number of areas from the perspective of an urban minister:

- transition from curacy to first post in an urban area;

- goal-setting;

- support structures and self-care;

- devotional life.

## Lifestyle: the way we are now

As I look at the Church in which I minister today, I am both encouraged and, sometimes, quite frankly, dismayed.

The *Faith in the City*[2] report drew widely on the experience of those who peopled our urban landscapes, a heady mix of stony realism mingled with hope based on the lived experience of congregations and priests, many of whom struggled hard to survive, many of whom also were sole glimmers of hope in communities decaying around them physically and structurally.

Those called to work on the outer housing estates and in inner-city parishes knew the joy of doing something meaningful and important there; many, though, also knew what it was to be crushed by the task.

And it looked as though the established Church was going to show some verve and imagination in addressing at least some of the issues that presented themselves. The areas in which I first worked as an assistant and in which I now continue to work as parish priest saw significant human and financial resources turning their way – and such resourcing often did bear fruit in increased numbers in congregations (or at least helped stem the haemorrhage of people), and the availability of central church funding facilitated more usable and sustainable church buildings for the benefit of a wider community. The Church was seen to be a viable partner with the politicians, and in the case of the Church of England one of very few 'honest brokers' with no particular axe to grind. The parish system also meant that we remained where many other more independent systems of church life and organization had already left.

But from where I stand 18 years after ordination, the vision seems to have dimmed as the Church of England takes financial and numerical stock of its position. I do not believe that inner-city and outer housing estate parishes (often by definition some of the poorest areas of our country) are likely to thrive well in this new climate. They seldom have lay leadership that can take on tasks from the priests who, ironically in the light of *Faith in the City*'s urgent recommendations, will be missing from the ground. They do not have the financial clout to meet the increasing demands of the Church to make up what is lacking in funding from central sources. The clustering, grouping or teaming of parishes in the city setting (which now mirrors what has for long been the case in the countryside) is unlikely to serve the city any better than it has the countryside.

Nonetheless, I find myself sustained by the reality of my own day-to-day and long-term experience. I have had the joy of being part of a 'success story' – being a priest on an outer city housing estate where the Church has regained an increasingly important place in the life of the community, and where numbers have grown steadily over the years such that the present worshipping congregation now numbers ten times that of a decade ago.

In much of our Church of England, beyond the stories of decline, there are equally stories of growth and faithfulness, often in unexpected places. I do recognize, though, that given the overall picture of numerical decline (or at best maintenance), every story that speaks of growth must also indicate that decline generally is perhaps more rapid and severe than most of us care to imagine. That is the blunt reality with which we are now living.

## Transition

At my licensing as priest-in-charge of a sprawling council estate, among the 'signs of ministry' presented to me during the liturgy was a helium balloon emblazoned with the text 'I'm in charge now'.

Equally this balloon might have read 'It's all my fault now' or perhaps, translated more positively, 'The responsibility is mine'. In a sense the balloon brought home that awesome charge laid upon a new incumbent by the bishop: 'Receive the cure of souls which is both mine and yours.' The bishop, however, was able to go home that night to another place.

For many curates their first post will have been a secure place in which to learn, experiment and develop (as long as the diocesan authorities have done their part in carefully choosing parishes and priests suitable as training posts and enablers). Organization and systems will probably have been part of the inheritance. Few are thrown in at the deep end completely without structure and support. The transition from a curacy can often be a move from such inherited and shared organization to a place of lone (and lonely) responsibility.

For example, one induction service in an urban area included the handing over by churchwardens of the keys to the church building. What the new incumbent, used to a different and more organized regime, did not realize was that on his first Sunday no one else would be there to open up for worship. The opening of doors, negotiating heating and lighting systems, arranging chairs, even putting the tea urn on, were all part of the new-found responsibility. Another priest found that all the duty rosters for the parish ended abruptly the Sunday before the induction service; the expected well-oiled machinery simply wasn't there, nor were the teams of people that had been part of the experience in the former suburban church.

The modern ideal of ministry is no doubt one of shared and mutual support between pastor, wardens, officers and people. In a first curacy that may well have been the established pattern. The move to a new sphere of ministry in a different social context may bring with it the realization that the people to whom you look for shared support may in fact be almost entirely dependent on you and not at the point at which they can assume responsibility. Indeed, wardens and officers may just have been longing for the day when they could hand back the responsibilities they have had to assume during an interregnum and for which they may believe they have neither aptitude nor ability.

Dependent on the social class of an urban parish, indigenous leadership may not be natural; it needs to be recognized that an Urban Priority Parish will be very different from one that is more middle class, both in terms of need and expectation. People with 'get up and go' will often do exactly that and, for the priest, cultivation of individuals for leadership positions may take a great deal of patience and may lead to frustrations and disappointments.

In one parish at a particularly low ebb, with only a handful of elderly people who had kept a declining show going, the new incumbent was able to take with him a number of very capable people from his former parish who were able to offer the leadership and skills that had been missing from the local situation. The unintended side-effect of this scenario, which introduced at one fell swoop a new, obvious and significant layer of 'more capable' people, was the creation of an eclectic congregation that did not really reflect or have lasting effect on the community in which that church was set. And while it may have made the incumbent's life more bearable to bring these folk with him, I dare to venture that it effectively de-skilled local people already burdened by their own sense of failure.

My own experience suggests that a better model is one where you can create a mix of local and imported leaders, which supplements local nous with missing skill – though I freely admit that there is a great balancing act to be attempted in the doing of this.

In the city there is a greater concept and facility of choice; even with all the mergers and closures of recent decades, the Church of England still has more local branches, after all, than most high street banks. And as with supermarkets, people will shop around for a style of church and worship that suits their need and taste. In the city there is consequently a greater opportunity to reflect and promote your own style of church tradition – evangelical, catholic or whatever. If people don't like what is on offer, they can and will move to the church down the road. The danger in this is that you can end up simply serving like-minded souls (and only mobile ones at that) rather than the whole parish within which your church is set. The significant advantage is that there needs to be less apology about your own particular style of worship. You can give it to them straight!

## Goals

After the launch into a new ministry, an important part of the game-plan needs to be the clear setting of goals and the sequential laying out of your vision. You need to do this in order to produce growth in both the short and long term. But until you have achieved your short-term plan, it is probably wiser to defer your long-term aims. See what is achievable, and start with small expectations. That way at least you won't be disappointed. You can then move your goal posts wider. Perhaps in the context of the leafy suburbs I would be saying something very different, but my own experience on a city estate makes me want to remain realistic at all times and thereby sustain hope rather than court depression.

But just how do you go about prioritizing tasks? Start from where you are. It is no use wielding new baptismal policies in a parish with virtually no baptisms. Some parishes may have several funerals a week; apart from the revenue (for which the diocese will be grateful), this may offer the weekly potential to touch the lives of hundreds who live in and around your parish with whom you would ordinarily have little or no contact.

You may have gifts in dealing with schools or with children. If school corporate worship becomes one of your priorities, it is important that schools know that they can normally depend on you not to cancel.

The enthusiasm of the priest in a new setting needs to be tempered by realism. A wise spiritual director, long used to urban working-class parishes, was able to reassure a younger colleague that in each parish in which he had ministered it was between three and four years before he saw any growth or evidence of change. For most of us, fresh to the task, that may seem an eternity.

Whatever else, there needs to be a balance between what we do in building up the community of faith and what we do for the wider community, the neighbour we are called to serve in Christ.

# Support

You will find it helpful to have a person or persons to act as a safe sounding board to bounce ideas off and assess how things are going. It needs to be understood that this may not always be available within the local congregation. It probably also needs to be someone other than your spiritual director. For once fortunate, the urban minister probably has more access to these resources close at hand than the country practitioner, and on occasion diocesan structures may be in place to facilitate this. Where I minister it has been for some time a condition of taking up an appointment in the urban context that the priest become part of either an inner- or outer-city ministry group for support, reflection, and the sharing of experience and expertise.

The Ordinal freely admits that 'you cannot bear the weight of this ministry in your own strength but only by the grace and power of God'. This dependence on God is certainly true but seldom enough; you also need others with whom to discuss both your ministry and yourself – people who will offer you their critical support and friendship. But be aware that this support will not always come from colleagues (if you have them). One training incumbent passed on to the curate the sage advice that colleagues may not always work with you to your best advantage; indeed they can sometimes undo what you have taken time to build up.

There is the (almost) amusing story of my cat, Luke, who developed severe behavioural problems. The sound of the phone or front door bell would send the cat into a frightened frenzy, destructively tearing round the house, and nothing I did would calm him down. The vet prescribed Valium (for the cat, not for me), which made things a little better but still not right. Eventually the vet suggested either a visit to an expensive animal psychologist or the purchase of a second cat to befriend the first. The second cat did the trick. By extension, this true tale simply suggests the life of the cat mirroring the destructive capability of loneliness and isolation that is so often the priest's lot in the urban wilderness.

Strategies for coping that are issued 'from above' may include suggestions about creating local ministry teams that include Readers and perhaps locally ordained or self-supporting ministers. It's a wonderful idea. But in nearly 20 years and in a variety of settings, I have known only one Reader in post and only a couple of lasting vocations to priesthood in the local setting (others may have gone on to stipendiary ministry, but that hardly helps – the wider Church's gain is most often the local church's loss). There is a naivety in thinking that the outer-estate or the un-regenerated inner-city provides a 'des res' home for retired clergy or those for whom non-stipendiary ministry is a viable financial option. While of course not universally true, many of those with get up and go will do just that, and the urban parish is not a natural breeding ground for the sort of book-led and book-bound ministry that the Church more broadly seems to think appropriate (perhaps an ironic comment in the latest book on ministry!). Desirable as it is, the creation of an 'indigenous' local ministry is likely to be more time-intensive in the urban setting than elsewhere and may require more local support than it might in another milieu. However, I know that my recent personal experience of helping a local candidate grow in confidence and to make the move from pew to pulpit has given me a great boost and a bit more freedom; the result is really worth the effort.

Where imported help mingles with local human resources (my preferred option, where available, in every case), such people may provide some of the team-type collegiality that is increasingly necessary, but I do believe that it is important to avoid the impression of a spiritual or even practical elite. Interestingly one former colleague, who had become stressed out, went to his doctor for help and discovered an equally stressed person on the other side of the desk; for them that meeting was an important starting point for mutually supportive help over a number of years. In my own area a regular lunchtime meeting of professionals in the community (teachers, police, health carers and others) provided a forum where common issues might be pursued; but like so much in already over-weighty diaries the sustainability of this relies heavily on the input of a few enthusiasts.

I have heard of clergy, not wanting the securities (or stresses) of a formal team, using clerical neighbours as sounding boards and supports, and there are groupings of the like-minded, Catholic and Evangelical, that aim to provide a support structure for one another.

However it is is done, this issue of isolation really does need to be addressed, particularly as the Church struggles with the financial implications of sustaining the ordained ministry. Most dioceses are responding by cutting their clergy establishment figures. Even where team or group ministries have been set up or are now being established, the immensity of the task each individual must undertake, as the area they have to cover expands, means that much will necessarily be done alone. And sadly, there is the danger that only the most independent and rock-solidly-sure individuals will be able to cope in this new environment. Few of us are that sure of ourselves, and we need the support of others. I hope that I have indicated one or two strategies that may help, but there really is a great deal of room yet for creative thinking on this front.

# Health and safety at work

One of the effects of mobility and shifting populations in the city is that these days it is often unreasonable to expect those who live within the boundaries of your parish to know where the church is or in which parish they live; so, when being asked to conduct funerals, weddings or baptisms, don't expect to be asked for either by name or by parish.

This lack of a settled and static community can almost inevitably lead to conflicts with neighbouring clergy, many of whom are frustrated by the dividing lines between parishes that would stop them fishing beyond their boundaries; if ordinary people do not recognize the parish boundaries, why should they? So, while you can establish the finest baptismal policy for the well-being of parish and people, your neighbours may not always respect or understand this. As the 'new kid on the block' your lack of experience (and your neighbour's greater knowledge) may be cited against you. The vaunted and much cherished independence of the Anglican parish can sometimes work against your best-laid kingdom priorities.

So it is important to establish where your parish begins and ends – you need to know your parish even if others don't. I have discovered that even after 13 years in one place, having performed a huge number of funerals, weddings and baptisms, many people who live in the parish still don't know who I am.

Even being successful (whatever that may mean) can make you enemies. Do not believe that fellow clergy are impervious to the Green Eyed Monster! Relative success in others can be perceived by some as threat; I suppose that if you are struggling in a similar situation, and someone appears to be doing 'better' than you, your own level of fear or guilt is potentially increased. And, on the other hand, if you are 'doing well' yourself, do you really want the competition? Even the appreciative hierarch who recognizes your good points and sings your praise ('If only all my priests were more like . . .') may unintentionally cause you to become the *bête noire* of your peers.

Success can make the pressure of your own work worse, for you risk constantly having to battle in order to maintain your position and feed your own expectations – as a friend said to me, you have to keep your foot on the gas pedal at all times. Type-casting sets in too, for if you have proved yourself good in one setting, it often seems that all you are then offered is more of the same. I guess it's a bit like the actor who makes a hit of a particular role in a TV serial; the other roles then tend to dry up. But it really does need to be borne in mind that, because of the personal cost involved, we may only be able to perform one big task in the course of a whole ministry.

## Security

One of the things you may not expect from your ministry is to be physically abused. The simple fact is that attacks on clergy in their own homes and in the places they work are frequent and increasing. In recent years we have already seen the murder of a couple of urban clergy, and on my own patch three of us were attacked in the same week by one individual well known to us.

As possibly the only professional carer left in your community at evening and weekend (for example, teachers, doctors and social workers tend to live away from where they work), we can be sitting targets for aggression and hurt. Your own security is important and it is not unreasonable to insist that diocesan authorities take your security seriously (many do); adequate lighting, security alarms, panic buttons, peepholes, and internal doors between front door and the rest of the house – yes, these may be expensive but they are no longer unreasonable. Don't let anyone tell you they are.

You need to learn how to be streetwise in terms of your own physical safety. Do not carry around or keep in the house large amounts of money (for example, bank funeral fees regularly), and do not put yourself in a vulnerable position. While hospitality is important, show caution in allowing people into your home, in how you answer the door and where you leave your car. In the house it is probably best to keep expensive or vulnerable property out of sight.

While always hoping and looking for the best, be prepared for the worst. My own experience has been that when I have been off guard and too relaxed, those have been the occasions when I have actually suffered personal injury. The sweet and elderly caller at the door asking for a financial handout can easily turn into a violent and dangerous person when they don't get quite what was asked for.

In the city it is more than likely that there will be a number of churches in the one locality and often your 'on the road caller' will be on a regular route, calling in on all the local religious houses of the area. It may be good to establish a phone-chain to warn other local ministers of the presence on the patch of any person likely to cause them harm or hassle.

## The priest and God

Priests are called by God to work ... as servants and shepherds among the people to whom they are sent. They are to proclaim the word of the Lord, to call hearers to repentance and in Christ's name to absolve and declare the forgiveness of sins. They are to baptize, and prepare the baptized for Confirmation.

> **They are to preside at the celebration of the Holy Communion.**
> **They are to lead the people in prayer and worship,**
> **to intercede for them, to bless them.**

The Ordination Service makes it clear that prayer and worship are integral to ministry. I suppose it should really go without saying that the priest should be a person of prayer. But without colleagues to pray with, spiritual life can be put on the back burner, something to be done later. All of us, without exception, need to develop a rule of life appropriate to our urban setting.

No longer in the shelter of the walled garden that was theological college or course, and no longer able to take refuge under another's routine, we have to set up a sustainable regime in our particular setting for prayer and spiritual reading. It is a simple matter of fact that things like prayer must be fitted in around the other invariables with which we contend daily – whether that is having to be available for schools or undertakers from 9.00 a.m. onwards, meetings during the evening, or dropping-off or collecting your children at school. If prayer is to be a priority, it requires and deserves a clear time-slot that will not conflict with other equally defined priorities or with rush-hour traffic.

Similarly we must not be afraid to claim the time necessary for quiet days and reflection, without which we risk becoming arid and unfruitful. For many of us this will mean finding a place outside home and parish, and away from phone and doorbell, where this can be claimed. There are a number of Religious Communities, Anglican and Roman Catholic, in or within easy reach of the urban jungle who will freely offer hospitality and space to parish clergy in need of quiet and renewal whether for a day or longer. And while we will all claim we cannot spare the time, an annual period of retreat is a helpful discipline.

On that subject of discipline, one diocesan bishop asked the newly ordained what form they used for Morning and Evening Prayer. He discovered a variety of usage but also an almost total lack of use of the Daily Office among one or two. A busy man himself, he cautioned the need for discipline. His own experience was that if he did not say Morning Prayer before breakfast it was likely to remain unsaid.

The Prayer Book requires 'the curate' (quaint language for the incumbent of a parish) to toll the church bell before the saying of Mattins and Evensong. While the ringing of a bell can occasionally invite phone calls about nuisance, it is more often construed by the people who live within its hearing that their priest is at work – and that prayer is no less work than visiting or being seen around the community.

My own experience has been that the Prayer Book's requirement can serve as a useful reminder that physically entering into the 'sacred space' of the church building is an important part in maintaining a disciplined spirituality. It is also my observation that the habit of saying the Office in the warmth of an office or study can become lax and die; there are, after all, usually more pressing things to get done.

Saying the Offices alone is hard. The experience of college or course and of the training parish will have been of sharing daily worship with others, and this move to worshipping only with the angels can be a difficult one to handle and sustain. But even if lay people have time and opportunity to join you, this too can become a hindrance or even form what may be perceived by self or others as a spiritual elite.

I am by nature an activist, yet I believe that there is a real need to balance prayer and activity. Occasionally one hears the comment that a priest has a 'ministry of being', not one that is task led, and there is a sense in which this is true. It can also be an excuse simply not to be doing anything. Prayer, however, has been described as usefully doing nothing with God.

## Lifestyle

'In the good old days' you might have expected to be accorded a place of respect in the community almost as an automatic right of being the parson (did people even in the 1940s really move from pavement to gutter in one working class parish to allow their parish priest to pass by?).

You may find this still to be the case in your particular setting. But the opposite is more likely, and you will have to win a place in structures and in other people's thinking.

One Saturday evening, while I was doing my shopping, a woman tapped me on the shoulder. I assumed (I was wearing a clerical collar and my usual black attire) that she was local, had recognized me, and wanted to ask a question about getting banns read, or having a child christened. No, for some reason she had the impression that I was the store assistant, and wanted to know where the tomatoes were. That put me in my place. You can't even assume that people will know what you are, let alone where you are from. By virtue of the size and diverse nature of an urban setting, there is often a sense in which the priest is anonymous, no longer recognized even by the uniform. With increasing secularization people will not know what a priest is, let alone how to treat them.

> One colleague of mine went into one of the local primary schools. The first question to him from kids in the playground was not 'Who are you?' but 'What are you?' He tried explaining that he was from the church (which was a matter of 100 metres from school). The next question was 'What is a church?' Youngsters, who probably played on a corner near the church, had no conception of what that building was. That's the base line from which we are starting.

## Shopping, schools and surgeries

There is a sense in which it is the priest who is called to a life of service, not the rest of the family. But the rest of the family (if you have one) inevitably have to bear some of the cost and sacrifice that goes with ministry.

You may find that on your patch you have a limited or even a poor choice of schooling for your children. The quality of healthcare – doctors, dentists and other professionals – may well be poorer in particular urban settings.

The choices you make about local schooling for your children will be open for scrutiny almost as much as those made by any Prime Minister or Minister for Education. The way you go about seeking knowledge of local educational standards, your desire to obtain the best for your children, and even the eventual choice of a particular school for them over and against others, leaves you open potentially to being a cause of offence.

Shopping in your local community may be an important lifestyle choice that allows you to become more easily recognized and helps in the building up of local relationships that may later impact upon your ministry. The down side is that this may be an expensive exercise because of the necessary economies of scale in the smaller setting, and a compromise too in terms of quality and/or choice. For me, regular shopping in the local area, rather than a trip to an out of town mall with greater choice and facilities, has led to many a conversation leading to baptism or marriage, or even opened up the long-buried grief of neo-natal death; in a sense, it has been one way of becoming 'their priest' rather than 'the priest'.

## Tail piece

If what I have said seems at all scary, it is. But then again, we were never promised an easy ride, simply an ultimate victory.

Occasionally I am asked why I still want to carry on as a priest when the world is indifferent to so much that I represent, and when the Church itself seems to regard me, and much of what I believe and hold dear, to a degree to be marginal. The reason is quite simply this: the people. Being allowed access into the lives of people at times of crisis and need, and in their day-to-day pilgrimage of faith, is a privilege that I continue to treasure.

On the night of his induction, a friend of mine was given three sheep (woolly toys rather than the real things); they were given as a reminder to him of the flock of Christ entrusted to his care that night. And it is that flock of Christ – the people – whose love keeps me going, for like so many other clergy I find that my ministry is as much trial as blessing. In them I see the face of God, sometimes pained, sometimes radiantly joyful. It is my hope that through me, despite my faults and failings, they too may find something of eternal value in a transitory world. I have never really understood why God called me, rather than someone else, to be his priest. But I am glad.

# Rural ministry

Jennifer Zarek

## Why rural ministry?

There are, of course, as many answers to that question as there are people asking it. The priest considering a move into rural ministry can find a lot of helpful information available from the Arthur Rank Centre for Rural Ministry at Stoneleigh (which runs short introductory courses) and the Rural Theology Association;[3] and the fact that such material exists makes the point that there are real distinguishing characteristics in ministry, as well as in the rural environment.

Environment is a matter of personal preference. You know for yourself whether you are happiest with greenery, a bit of mud, the incredible racket of a field of young lambs, and the opportunity to examine in detail the rear view of a combine harvester in a narrow lane, or with sodium street lights and the sound of a tin can being kicked along the gutter. There are aspects of rural ministry that can be equally matters of preference and temperament – and of vocation. Writing of *Ministry in the Countryside* in 1994, Andrew Bowden commented that 'there is a parson-shaped hole at the centre of every parish'.[4] To the extent that this remains true (and it does, more than in urban areas), it is both the privilege and the problem of rural ministry, and the source of many conflicts between the desires and expectations of parishioners and the realities of the Church today.

While rural areas may be perceived as trying to live in the past, it is they that are being forced most immediately into change. Bishops often relate how at confirmations, they comment to a churchwarden who has held the post for several decades that 'You must have seen a lot of changes', and receive the reply 'Yes – and I've opposed them all'. But rural areas are leading the thinking that will increasingly impinge on the urban and suburban, responding to the decline in numbers of stipendiary clergy, the unsustainable burden of maintenance of buildings no longer suitable for their use, a church having to pay for itself today rather than being subsidized by the Church of yesterday, and a wider population that sees a 'service on demand' rather than a 'parson-shaped' hole in its community. The rural backwater is in fact the place for innovative thinking – although innovative action may be a little less immediate – and not for a quiet life!

## The rural church community

People are probably much the same everywhere; but the structural differences between the Church and ministry in urban and rural contexts may now be greater than at any time in the past. Changes driven by the needs (primarily financial, but also theological) of the wider institution are not willingly embraced by local congregations, and although much is being thought, written and done to learn how to operate multi-parish benefices, the history and assumptions of rural parishes always make amalgamation problematic and there is a practical limit to how far it can be taken.

Congregations are usually supremely unconcerned with bright ideas of how good it might be to amalgamate their administration, let alone their worship. 'I'm not interested in what happens in the rest of the benefice, let alone abroad', asserted one deanery synod member in response to a diocesan proposal for overseas twinning. The persistent tendency to congregationalism is particularly evident in financial matters, in which the idea remains (usually because it has not been challenged by past incumbents) that 'the Church' is a rich institution which sends (and pays for) the vicar who does the work of the Church in the parish, and that money raised locally should be devoted to the running of local church building.

One of the biggest issues that you as the new incumbent will need to understand, and which  the wider church should also recognize, is just *how* small a rural congregation can be, and how limited its resources. The work of Springboard and other practitioners of 'healthy church' development is useful in assisting parishes to discover for themselves the nature of church community.[5] but their material must be applied carefully to your context. Diocesan and central bodies, whatever their goodwill and good intentions, consistently fail to understand circumstances in which it may not be possible to find churchwardens; in which one person may be warden, PCC secretary and PCC treasurer; in which it is almost impossible to pay the insurance premium, let alone parish share; in which there are no facilities or human resources even to make tea, let alone run a crêche; where a photocopier (never mind a computer) is regarded as strange; and where they ran out of personnel to run a fund-raising fête a decade ago. But – and this is the big 'but' of rural ministry – the devotion of generations of worshippers continues. You are not the only one who can feel depressed rather than encouraged by enthusiastic stories of 'good practice', which illustrate just what can *not* be done. And you will not be the first vicar to realize that whatever our lip-service to lay ministry, your congregation lacks the critical mass, energy, resources and experience suddenly (or even gradually) to take on for themselves things that have always been done for them.

Despite, or because of, these limitations, rather than trying to limit amalgamation, some more radical thinking is suggesting *wider* amalgamation into clusters, some taking the historical model of the Minster or the contemporary model of the doctor in general practice into collaboration across the area of a deanery, centred in the market town and with outposts in the villages. Pooling of the leadership of clergy, Readers and even wardens could make good use of resources while supporting local centres of worship – even if posing a headache in terms of legalities! While the response of congregations to such suggestions is likely to be that 'they won't like it' (the criterion for judging many things is the predicted response of 'they' rather than the owned response of 'we'), some of these more radical (and sometimes informal) experiments have received wholehearted support from congregations – sometimes because they are perceived as getting one over on a hierarchy that is thought to be prescriptive and remote, although sometimes because they are perceived as an interim measure before getting back to old ways.

## The rural congregation

The statistical characteristics of the rural church are of small congregations – although representing a larger proportion of the population than in urban areas – usually ageing, often finding it difficult to pay their parish share and usually finding it impossible properly to maintain a historic building. This is the background, but for you as the minister the more influential differences are less the physical and sociological setting than the history and the continuing assumptions preserved by the congregation. Many people living in villages in an agricultural landscape are more truly part of a dispersed suburbia than of a rural community. Genuinely agricultural or rural communities are rare, since working on the land and with livestock employs very few people. Where there does remain a community formed by common occupation, it is dispersed among a population whose means of livelihood are those of any urban dweller. Whether by choice or necessity (the scarcity of shops, schools, doctors and other facilities) everyone travels for their choice of shopping, employment, schooling, leisure and entertainment, and needs a car (a clergy family must almost certainly budget for two cars). The (non) availability of transport is a hidden but vital issue. However it is truly said that the same people will not travel to church, and it must be recognized that even by travelling, choices are limited. There may only be one supermarket serving the area; and the parish church may have to be all things to all Christians. We cannot please all of the people all of the time. An uneasy truce may have reigned for generations between those who don't like 'this nasty communion stuff that the vicar keeps foisting on us' and those who cannot see the point of Sunday worship that is *not* eucharistic, and the assumptions of those steeped in the history of a rural community are different from those of the newly dispersed suburban residents. These differences must be clearly recognized if the threat of terminal decline is to be converted into a situation of sustainable Christian presence. You will be well advised to recognize what a can of worms may be opened by any questioning of, or adjustment to, patterns of worship. Those who do not like what is on offer cannot shop around between parishes and denominations as they might in urban areas, and remain to fight fiercely for their own tastes.

## John Clarke: rural and 'incomer' Christianity

Today's rural community is not monochrome. It is a blend of settled community and those who have moved in more recently. An analysis of characteristics which distinguish between the 'rural' and the 'urban' or 'incomer' church has been offered by John Clarke of the Arthur Rank Centre.[6] While any schematic generalization can generate discussion, this summary could usefully be pinned above the desk or on the fridge door of every rural incumbent.

| | RURAL CHURCH | URBAN and INCOMER CHURCH |
|---|---|---|
| The source of the congregation | Community | Associational |
| Basis of faith | Custom, 'folk' religion | Doctrinal |
| Relationship between people and Church | Church belongs to people | People belong to Church |
| Boundaries | Blurred edges | Sharp edges |
| Basis of membership as a Christian | (Self) identification | Participation in the Church |
| Qualification for membership | Ethics – to be Christian is to be a good neighbour | Salvation experience |
| Primary creed | Belief in God. Creation – that which is given | Faith in Jesus. Redemption – forgiveness |
| Behaviour | Sobriety A personal and *private* faith, tested by conduct | Enthusiasm A personal and public faith, involving witness |
| Motivation | Belief in God (which might cost nothing) | Following Christ (which might be costly) |
| Liturgical preference | *Book of Common Prayer* | *Common Worship* (the theology of an associational Church) |

(Clarke was speaking in the time of the *ASB*, but *Common Worship* follows the same pattern.)

In addition to Clarke's distinguishing features, in many places we might now add, following Robert Warren (*Being Human, Being Church*),

| Model of the Church | 'Roman', parochial, locally centred | 'Celtic', missionary |
|---|---|---|
| Future outlook | unsustainable | possibly sustainable |

# Working with the rural church

Dom John Chapman famously advised 'pray as you can, and do not try to pray as you can't'. Whatever the sphere of ministry, most of us need reminding to minister with who we are, not who we are not; and it can be a useful maxim in shaping ministry, to work with who we have and not with who we have not. Strategies then come under three headings:

- the way in which the priest ministers;

- the modelling of the benefice as an entity and within the structure of the Church;

- the prioritization of ministerial work within the benefice.

## The pattern of ministry

The way in which any individual does a job is a negotiation between all three factors, the result is determined by the person as much as by the context, and every answer is different. Perhaps the greatest danger lies in looking at models, the 'good ideas' and best practice seen in other people and other places, and assuming that all of them are necessary and possible.

The difficulties that you will face are those faced by every parish priest, but prioritization, multi-tasking, delegating and, above all, deciding what *not* to do, are inevitably more acute in a multi-parish context. In prioritizing and selecting, an objective analysis of the reality (easier for some temperaments than others!) is invaluable as a personal tool and – even more so – as a tool for communication and discussion. Many clergy pay lip-service to the notion of long hours and demanding tasks, but even so if they actually log their work, they are astonished at the results. PCCs are even more astonished. If objective facts are presented, unrealistic expectations are, at least, challenged, and it is possible that collaborative action can develop better patterns. It may never have occurred to PCC members that you have sat through the same discussions at several meetings. Perhaps joint meetings can discuss common questions of worship and mission, and separate meetings (at which you do not always need to be present) can discuss the gutters and the lawnmower. PCC members have even less idea of what you may be doing when not publicly visible. The kindly meant 'you mustn't do too much, vicar' tends to mean 'say no to those others, but do what we want'. PCCs can be invited – challenged – to join you in looking at what really can be done, and who needs to do it. Gradually, they may begin to see themselves as participants in, as well as recipients of, ministry.

## The pattern of the benefice

In respect of the benefice, there can be a lack of clarity at both diocesan level and at parochial level as to quite what a 'benefice' means, and a considerable reluctance to engage with the question. For incumbents and their parishes, the changes of recent years have left us with a fundamental choice. Amalgamation has usually resulted in a pattern of services that does not offer an act of worship in every parish every week. It is a universal observation that very few people travel elsewhere when there is no service in 'their' church, and fewer still feel the necessity to organize their travels in order to make a weekly communion. This breaking of the pattern of a weekly commitment to worship ('There wasn't a service last week, so why should I bother to go this week when I want to go shopping, visit grandma, have a day out . . .') may be the biggest single factor in the decline of active church membership in such parishes. We – people and priest – can choose either to pursue the 'rationalization' route or, while it may not be too late, to recover the centrality of the local church community. There are signs of a U-turn in policy about the leading of worship, and an encouragement of the emergence of lay worship leaders (including, by virtue of their office, churchwardens), who may be assisted by the incumbent in planning a service and given a sermon or other material to read in the 'sermon slot'. It can be instructive (for both parties) for you to ask your congregations what they really want: is it, in fact, weekly worship for which they may have some responsibility (and if not, why not?) or only the fortnightly or monthly visit made by you as priest or by a Reader? And remember that we need not assume that the worship takes place in a cold, leaky ancient monument rather than a farmhouse kitchen. On this may hang many other decisions about the structure and the work of the benefice, which can be rooted in the reality of what congregations actually want. Whatever the answer, the encouragement of lay worship leadership may have a profound effect on the self-image of the congregation – not least in realizing that perhaps there is less of a 'parson-shaped hole' in their midst than they had thought – and on the welfare of the incumbent. Ron Wood writes of Lay Worship Leadership: 'Once a month, if you have a vicar, encourage him or her to leave the LWL to do a service and go off to hear a colleague lead worship, and listen to someone else preach. (I know vicars who haven't heard a sermon for years!)'[7]

## The work of the Church

Faced with the obvious truth that our congregations tend to be older and ageing, the Church as a whole is putting effort and resource into youth work. While some criticism of this as producing no measurable long-term effect may be overstated, as a matter of practicality our rural churches usually need to be concerned and genuinely engaged with the spiritual welfare of older people.

In all honesty, this may also be more the natural milieu of many clergy. The spiritual nurture and care of older people needs expertise, just as does that of young people, and insight and resources are available from specialists such as the Leveson Centre for the Study of Ageing, Spirituality and Social Policy.[8] There may be more purpose in concern for the nurture of the people who are in our congregations than of those who are not. This is not to diminish concern for those many individuals who seek the ministry of the church in occasional offices and other times of need, nor for offering stepping stones to church membership, but to look at where to make most investment of stretched resources.

There may be (Clarke's 'rural' model) a lot of resistance to what clergy consider to be spiritual growth; but equally there are those − maybe few − who seize an encouragement that they have not had before, and blossom visibly. These are the people who have the potential to show a real and lively faith to the enquirers who may, just occasionally, turn up in our churches, and in our current circumstances, these are the people who are the evangelists.

## The need to be 'bi-lingual'

As a result of its community rather than associational character, the rural church is often more strongly wedded to the 'Roman', territorial and institutional model than is the urban church; yet in rural areas it is most clear that current structures are already unworkable. Clergy in rural parishes need to be aware of which of Clarke's patterns more accurately represents their own theology, experience and motivation. It is likely that whatever our origin, by virtue of our training, exposure to critical thought about the nature of the Church, and the personal commitment which has led to ordination, most clergy identify with the 'incomer' model. This is, emphatically, not to say that the clergy and the incomers are right and the rural model is wrong. As Clarke insists, both are needed for the fullness of the gospel and the Church (rural and urban) needs to be 'bilingual'. But the first step towards tackling the problems created by either model must be that of recognizing its deficiencies. None of the problems that exist in rural churches is unique to them; but some are exacerbated by the situation.

## Population size

While the most obvious controlling factor in the life of a rural church congregation is its (lack of) size, it remains true that *as a proportion of the population* church attendance is actually higher in rural than in other areas, but there is frequently a critical mass problem. The size of the congregation is small in absolute terms. Clarke's analysis gives clues to the other major difficulty facing the rural church: the demands made on it by those who do not see any need to offer it commensurate support. Even more than in the urban church, there is the expectation that the Church is there when required, because it is visibly, physically and historically a centre of the village, and even 'because I pay my taxes'; but there is little acceptance of any right by the church to define what constitutes membership.

## The role of the vicar

There remains a high – and explicit – expectation, among both the congregation and the wider community that the vicar is entirely and solely responsible for the work of the church. Where the 'urban' model has usually been influenced by a laity who have their own capabilities, the rural church congregation, because of the low importance attached to its personal understanding of doctrine and faith, has perceived itself as unqualified to 'be' the church. While there are demonstrably situations in which there is active resistance to teaching and to opportunities for growth in faith ('What are Galatians?' asked a churchwarden, being given the reference for a Sunday reading over the phone), beware of attaching blame to congregations that behave in this way. In general, we are reaping the fruit of that which has been sown and carefully tended by our predecessors: the desire, need and training of the clergy to do everything themselves. Unfortunately clericalism, once a problem of the clergy and occasionally resisted by the laity, has often become a problem of the laity, desperately being challenged by the clergy. Two gloomy ladies offer as the reason for their refusal to receive communion at all in the presence of a lay chalice assistant, that 'The vicar's paid to do it; she should do it herself'.

As priest you must, of course, be a leader and (as far as permitted!) an enabler; you need also to be a listener. Clergy frequently make the comment of rural benefices that the greatest need is a growth in personal spirituality, but the truth of that comes from the 'incomer' model. The suggestion of Clarke's analysis is that there is another dimension. Clergy, and those of the 'incomer' school, may well agree with one another on the importance of the characteristics of Jesus / salvation / redemption in faith; but we may be missing something of a faith that is characterized by God / creation; and that is reminiscent of the Celtic spirituality that is enjoying a strong revival of interest.

Your challenge as a rural minister is to nourish existing values and insights while developing a structure that is sustainable. This may involve supporting rather than radically changing that which exists, and planting new seeds alongside. This is an important lesson for any minister – it is the rural church that may already be discovering and creating the shape of the Church of England for generations to come.

# Multi-parish benefices

Roger Morris

## Introduction

My aim in this section is to focus more closely on the Church's mission and ministry in a multi-parish benefice and to develop in more detail points already outlined in the previous section. I will examine some models of multi-parish benefices and consider some of the challenges that are peculiar to them. I will also explore strategies that apply to all models and discuss how to handle the first few months in post, how to identify and relate to the key players, how to work with the PCCs and how to meet the challenge of providing regular, lively and accessible worship.

These insights come, not from academic study, but from the personal experience of running a group of nine churches in Gloucestershire for the best part of seven years.

## Models of a multi-parish benefice

For parishes in a multi-parish benefice, structure is very important. The structure defines how the parishes should relate and also how the benefice should be managed.

The situation in which you, as a new rural incumbent, will find yourself will vary according to how people choose to balance what can be done locally with what must be done together. This is not an issue that will be resolved immediately, but it is one with which most multi-parish benefices will wrestle on an almost day-to-day basis. Some will call for greater centralization, whereas others would only grieve for what they feel they have lost. Clear structures, a common vision and the right style of leadership are vital.

Essentially there are three models of how churches in a multi-parish benefice might relate to one another. They are the Federal or Circuit model, the Minster model, and the Hybrid model. Below, I will be outlining each model and highlighting its particular challenges.

## The 'Federal' or 'Circuit' model

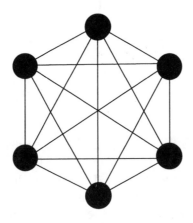

This model applies to a group of parishes in which none is clearly dominant in size. The benefice will probably have less than 2,000–3,000 inhabitants spread across villages of less than 500 each. In reality, the parish in which the incumbent lives will always dominate to some extent but steps must be taken to ensure that all parishes are seen as equal. It is of particular importance for you, as a new rural incumbent, to spread yourself evenly and to avoid appearing to show favour to some communities but not others. It is therefore advisable to make the most of every opportunity to raise your public profile across the benefice. This can be achieved by shopping in all the village shops, visiting all the local hostelries and also by gaining invitations to as many different community groups as possible. Occasional events such as farm dispersion sales can also provide a new incumbent with an excellent opportunity to meet people and to be seen.

Some parishes may enjoy a more specialized ministry. For example, one might become a 'stronghold' of the *Book of Common Prayer* whereas another, by virtue of the building's flexibility or the demography of the parish (or even the presence of toilet facilities), may choose to focus on work among children and young people.

There are many similarities between this model and the concept of the circuit that is the basic structure of the Methodist Church. The circuit meeting is made up of elected and ex-officio members and it combines spiritual leadership with administrative efficiency to help the circuit fulfil its purpose. The purpose of the circuit is to ensure that the resources of ministry, which include people, property and finance, are used effectively. The circuit acts as the focal point for the fellowship of the local churches and co-ordinates their pastoral care, training, and evangelistic work. The important lesson to take from Methodism is that the basic structure is not the chapel but the circuit. So the benefice and not the parish church must become the principal structure of which the individual churches are then seen as constituent parts. Energy needs to be directed towards creating and deepening a sense of belonging to the benefice. The real task is to encourage a shift in thinking from the parochial (which will be endowed with a sense of nostalgia for a mythical 'golden age' of the church) to a new way of working in which the Benefice becomes the foundational structure of the rural church.

## Keys to success

There are key steps one can take in order to promote this shift in perception from the primacy of the parish to a more benefice-focused church. One important step is to name the benefice (for example, after a river, an estate, etc.) rather than refer to it by listing the constituent communities as if they were the stops on a railway journey. Involving key people in this task will ensure a wide sense of 'ownership' of the new name. Having named the benefice, it is then useful to begin working towards a shared sense of purpose or vision statement to which all parishes can give their full backing. This can be a painful process in which the individualism of particular parishes is set at odds with the sense of 'being in this together'.

Among the more important vehicles for mission and outreach in a rural benefice is the church magazine. The first thing to ensure is that the benefice produces just one magazine covering all the villages. One group of parishes ran a regular monthly feature in which the spotlight was placed on each village in turn. Accompanying the article on the village's history was an invitation to morning coffee or afternoon tea at their church. This allowed people to travel around the villages and also learn something about them.

There is much that can be achieved by working in partnership with other institutions and agencies that cover the same area as the benefice (e.g., schools, shops, Age Concern, Royal British Legion, etc.). It may be worth negotiating with the other agencies and institutions so that they adopt the same grouping of communities and use the same name in referring to them. Some agencies even employ community outreach workers whose role often complements some of the social roles of the clergy and lay leadership. Close liaison with these agencies can be hugely beneficial to the church's ministry.

A vital ingredient in this process of moving towards a 'Federal Model' is the identification, training and support of a locally based ministry (either resourced by a team or by a small number of carefully selected individuals). Most dioceses now have 'Lay Ministry Teams' or 'Ministry Leadership Teams' that are made up of people who have the support and trust of the communities they serve. Such teams may also identify particular candidates for ordination (perhaps as Ordained Local Ministers).

The shift in thinking from 'parish mode' to 'benefice mode' is not easy and may take many years to bring about. There may be some value in employing a work consultant to accompany the benefice through this process (at least at the early stages when a move from a purely pastoral ministry to a ministry of oversight and administration may lead to the incumbent being accused of dereliction of duty).

## The 'Minster' model

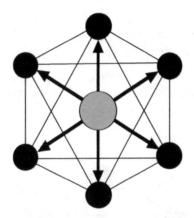

The Minster model is a way of structuring a benefice so that the larger church (the Minster) serves its own and satellite churches by providing additional resources to promote evangelism, the recruitment and training of local leadership, a consistent programme of teaching for all ages, and a coordinated and effective ministry of pastoral care. Such a structure can provide a richer and more effective church life at all levels.

### Keys to success

If your benefice discerns that it is right to move towards a Minster model then the first step to take is to build up and equip the Minster team. There may in fact be many Minster teams meeting centrally (but working in their local situations). Such teams might be the clergy team (including NSM, OLM, etc.), the Readers (who may join with clergy as 'Ministers of the Word'), the Wardens (who may have a leadership role, a liturgical role or a pastoral role within their own churches and parishes), a leadership team (this could be a benefice council), a pastoral team, a team working with children and young people, an evangelism and nurture team (running Alpha, co-ordinating Bible Study Groups, etc.), a team covering issues of social justice (including Christian Aid), or a meeting of parish treasurers.

It is important to site all the administration at the Minster church and you will want to give serious thought to the appointment of a part-time administrator. All registers can be stored together in the one safe at the Minster (which makes searches and diocesan returns easier) and each parish, officer, minister and warden can have a pigeon hole at the Minster office from which their correspondence can be picked up.

When working towards a Minster model, it is important to stress that the structure being adopted is very different from what was in place before. The housing of clergy in villages rather than at the centre, the holding of church meetings in places other than at the Minster and the duplication of Minster focused activities in the parishes can all give the mistaken impression that things have not altered and that the old structures have remained.

The crucial thing to remember is that the role of the Minster church is a missionary one in that it is a church that 'sends out' rather than just draws in.

## The 'Hybrid' model

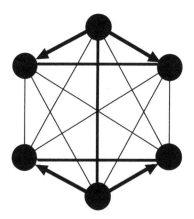

The 'Hybrid' model is effectively a federation of mini-Minsters. When large multi-parish benefices are formed from smaller benefices, there may well be two or three churches that, in their former smaller benefice, were the title parishes. For the first few years following such a reorganization, the former title parishes (with the exception of the one in which the incumbent resides) may feel a sense of loss and marginalization. The strength of such feelings may seriously hamper any efforts to organize the benefice along the lines of a Minster model. The 'Hybrid' model then becomes a useful transition phase.

In essence, the former title parishes become Minsters to the satellite parishes with which they were formerly linked. The two or three churches thus designated Minsters then form a federation with its own pooled resources and joined up administration. It must be stressed that this is a temporary model and not one to be established for the long term. It is the least efficient of all the models and it does little to develop the relationship between satellite churches that, prior to reorganization, were in separate benefices.

### Keys to success

If a Hybrid model fits your particular situation then this would tend to suggest that you allow either a Minister model or a Federal model to evolve gradually. If you are moving towards a Federal model then affirming the satellite churches and shifting the emphasis from the parishes to the benefice will help catalyse the process of change. If, however, you are moving towards a Minister model then the strategy would be gradually to join up certain activities and groups that are duplicated in each sub-group. This is a process of initiating one or two changes at a time, such as producing one parish magazine rather than two, or running one group for young people covering the whole benefice, or setting up one joint purchasing scheme for church requisites rather than each church or sub-group doing their own thing.

Whatever model you find yourself in or moving towards, there are certain isssues that are common to all. In what follows, I shall look at a few of these challenges and discuss strategies that might help to address them.

## New beginnings

Most pastoral reorganization takes place when clergy move on or retire. This means that many incumbents moving into a multi-parish benefice will be working with a newly formed cluster of parishes that will have no shared history. Many parishioners will be hoping that you, their new minister, will maintain the status quo and that, in this new arrangement of parishes, their own church will not lose out. The first job when faced with a new multi-parish benefice is to communicate the need to review how things are going. It is also crucial to invite people to join with you in this process of discernment and discovery. This process will inevitably lead to change.

## Timing

Rural churches tend to be quite conservative in style and many of their members will be those who value and protect tradition by opposing change in any form. Many incoming clergy try to appease such people by promising not to change anything for a fixed period of, say, six months. The difficulty with this approach is that people will find it hard to perceive any need for change given that their incumbent has managed to avoid changing things for the best part of a year. Other clergy will introduce a number of changes immediately but without appearing to show respect for what has gone before. Invariably, those who have taken an evolutionary approach to change often wish that they had been more revolutionary whereas those who adopted a revolutionary approach often wish that they allowed things to develop in a more gradual and evolutionary way. However you choose to manage change, it is important to view it as a process and then to commit yourself to the process as a whole. The early stages of the process will usually involve winning over the innovators and the early adopters. This is often the point at which some people feel that the job is done. It is not. Work then needs to be done in order to win over the late adopters who are naturally cautious and will need that extra little bit of convincing, either by the example of the early adopters or by the evidence of similar things working elsewhere.

Rural churches are often described as being 'Family-sized' because of the presence of one or two individuals or families who hold the power and to whom the incumbent is expected simply to act as chaplain. In the context of a 'Family-sized' church, change initiated in the first four or five years can often be seen as a challenge to the role and authority of these individuals and, given their durability compared with the more frequent comings and goings of parochial clergy, most people will choose not to support the incumbent and will therefore be resistant to change. Changing the culture and shape of the rural church will often take at least seven to ten years and success will often depend upon the backing and co-operation of these key individuals.

In many cases these key individuals will be churchwardens and this will provide you with a number of opportunities to meet with them in order to discuss the future direction and development of the benefice. Sometimes, however, these powerful figures will have either stood down from office or will have avoided such an obvious position of authority. If you have identified who these people are, then there is much to be gained from encouraging them to form a 'council of reference' to whom you can then look for support and advice.

Rural people may be conservative but there is often a real streak of pragmatism in them too. If what you propose is demonstrably good, then they may be won over more easily than you'd have thought. Once they have decided on something, rural people can also be quite quick to put it into practice. An individual may be very conservative about certain things but extraordinarily revolutionary about others. All this means that the process of change might run a lot more smoothly than you would otherwise have imagined.

# PCC meetings and administration

In a multi-parish benefice, some form of joint PCC meeting is essential. Such a meeting, often called the Benefice Council, aims to support local initiatives while also developing the church's ministry and mission across the whole benefice. The Benefice Council may have formal legal status or it may be informal. It may include wardens, members of a local ministry team, deanery synod representatives or PCC treasurers. By setting up such a meeting, it may then be possible for an incumbent to absent themselves from the odd PCC meeting of which, in a multi-parish benefice of 7 or 8 parishes, there could add up to 30–40 in a single year.

Another model proposed in Oxford Diocese sees the PCC membership stripped down to the minimum for administration, and a church warden placed in the chair. Prior to an ordinary meeting of the PCC, the warden who will be chairing the meetings meets with the incumbent in order to agree the agenda. This skeleton PCC is then expanded into a parochial meeting with the incumbent in the chair in order for the PCC to discharge its general responsibility to co-operate with the minister in 'promoting in the parish the whole mission of the Church, pastoral, evangelistic, social and ecumenical' [The Parochial Church Councils (Powers) Measure 1956]. All the church members on the electoral roll would be invited to one of these parochial meetings. A benefice meeting is then set up with the authority of the parishes (via the delegation of specific powers) so that issues of ministerial deployment, finance, pattern of services and communication can be addressed at a benefice level. A paid secretary is employed to function as administrator and co-ordinator in the benefice and as secretary to each of the PCCs. They are provided with a laptop computer with e-mail facility and are given the practical responsibility of maintaining communications within the congregation.

# Worship

When you tell people that you are the rector of seven, eight or nine churches, they immediately ask about Sunday and how you manage to run services in all those churches. You can't please all of the people all of the time and, in a multi-parish benefice, it is hard even to please some of the people some of the time.

Most multi-parish benefices work on a grid that says what's on in which church on any given Sunday. People who are adept at reading railway timetables find such a pattern easy, whereas others get confused by whether it is the third or fourth Sunday in the month and, by the close of the month, they have lost their copy of the parish magazine in which the grid can be found. Certain refinements to the grid can make life a little easier. One such refinement is to rationalize the times so that, for example, morning services are either at 8.00, 9.30 or 11.00. When looking at the times of services, it is important to allow some time for the person taking the service to stop and chat with the congregation before dashing off to take the next service.

Some benefices have chosen to have their main benefice service at the Minster church, and then hold smaller services at the satellite churches at times that do not clash with the benefice service. The benefice service is made all age and may include a Sunday school and crèche (facilities that might be unsustainable in the smaller satellite churches). The only setback with such a pattern is that the smaller services tend to be of a more traditional kind whose long-term popularity is in question. Therefore the Minster congregation would grow at the expense of the smaller satellite churches which might then become redundant.

Some benefices have agreed that, when a licensed minister is not available to take the service, a service of parish prayers is held, led by a member of the congregation. Training is given to the people leading the services and the content is kept at a basic level. At the very least, prayers are said and the Scriptures are studied (a little like one might expect in a cell or fellowship group).

## Buildings

It is the responsibility of the PCCs to examine critically the churches within the benefice and the ability of the benefice to maintain and sustain the buildings. They will need to look at and explore the market for alternative or additional uses for the church in the community.

Some churches in multi-parish benefices have, following alterations to their fabric, opened as a community facility or village hall. Often the chancel area (after re-ordering) proves sufficient for most services and the nave can then be cleared of ecclesiastical furniture and given over to community use. Some churches have converted the vestry or porch so that it can serve as the Post Office for the village. Post Offices can raise issues of security, especially in remote rural areas where they can be seen as easy targets by the criminal fraternity. However, the provision of such a service would massively enhance the church's role in the local community.

Another option might be to adapt one church for a more specific ministry such as children's work or youth work. One church could be the 'Sunday school room' for the whole benefice. If the cost of providing toilet facilities has proved to be too high for all the churches in a benefice, then working together to provide such facilities for the church specializing in children's ministry might be seen as an achievable goal.

If the benefice feels that it cannot sustain all the church buildings then it may have to identify one or more churches that should be considered for closure. It may not be difficult to identify such churches, but the decision to close them rests with the PCC of that church. This is a time for brave decisions that may be unpopular in the short term but, in the long term, they may lead to greater vibrancy in the church.

## Conclusion

When I became incumbent of nine churches in the Cotswolds, people often looked at me with a mixture of pity and concern. They would often ask, 'What help do you have?' which implied that they believed that the job was too much for one person. It was. However, I was not on my own. I had a number of people in each community with whom I was able to work and to whom I looked for support and advice. The rural church is not an organization that needs 'propping up' but it is a group of people who need releasing, enthusing and equipping so that, together with their incumbent, they can serve the purposes of God in the community in which God has placed them.

# 10

# Public ministry

## Preaching

Stephen Wright

I once heard a bishop commend a new incumbent to his congregation as 'a brilliant preacher'. I felt sorry for the incumbent concerned. For a start, he would have to live with the fear that the congregation would be disappointed. There would also have been the understandable temptation to rely on a supposed 'gift of preaching', and forget that the *way* in which a preaching gift should be exercised must always depend on careful listening to God and to one's context.

Writers and speakers on preaching often address the subject in the abstract, as if there were one identifiable kind of event that went by this name. However, many vital issues that pertain to preaching are not amenable to abstract, general treatment, but arise precisely from specific contexts.[1] This section focuses on questions about preaching that arise for the Christian minister (especially in the Anglican setting) when embarking on the overall pastoral charge of a church for the first time. I shall consider preaching in relation to different aspects of the minister's role: as representative, pastor, leader and human.

### The preacher as representative

> Our public speech as ministers is *representative*, not only of God, but also of the universal Church.[2]

This responsibility can at times feel burdensome, especially when you are the senior or sole pastor in a church. Yet to feel the representative nature of your preaching should also be releasing. It removes the pressure of always having to come up with something novel. Creativity is essential if preaching is to be engaging, but you don't have to create out of nothing. At the heart of preaching is the givenness of the faith handed down in Scripture, creed and Church. As you arrive in a new place of ministry, you do not come to share a privately revealed word, but to stand in the centre of a tradition, and to give fresh voice to it according to the needs of the times, the nature of your congregation, and the particular speech-gift entrusted to you.

Practically, this calls for a dynamic and flexible approach to sermon preparation, in which you are continually engaging with Scripture, theology and the world around you, building up a bank of material on which you can draw. All the time you must be open to the leading of the Spirit who guides you to the unique message you are to give on a particular occasion. I soon discovered that advice such as 'one hour preparation for every minute in the pulpit' was not only unnecessarily guilt-inducing, but also foreign to the nature of preaching. The crucial inspiration, the decision on the direction of the sermon, can often come in a flash, but availability for that moment is not engineered by sitting blankly for a certain length of time at a desk. Going for a walk, playing a piece of music, talking to a friend, routine pastoral visiting – these can all be ways in which your mind and spirit become receptive to the particular message God may have for you to speak.

It is especially at such times that the fundamental continuity and universality of the gospel should be a comfort. It doesn't matter repeating thrilling truth, as long as you don't give the impression that you are bored by it. Repeating sermon material may be particularly necessary when you have more than one church to serve. But 'repetition' should never descend into mere 'regurgitation': sensitivity to the particular character of the congregation and the occasion will always have an effect, however subtle, on your presentation.

At the other extreme from the over-conscientious preacher who draws too close a link between hours spent in the study and the effectiveness of the sermon is the preacher who thinks inspiration can replace preparation altogether. My heart sinks when a preacher tells us in their opening sentence that their message has just come to them as they were driving over to church (and yes, this happens). I have never yet found much profit from a sermon where the lack of prior thought about structure and even content is evident. Such preaching dishonours both God and the congregation, and becomes an embarrassing 'low' in the liturgy instead of an honourable 'high'. Once more, our representative calling to share the gospel should guide our practice. If we fail to think about how we are going to present it, we become trivial, eccentric or incoherent as its advocates.

The mechanics of how to fit sermon 'thought' into a busy week will vary from one person and situation to another. However, there is no excuse for not giving this significant public aspect of our ministry a high priority. Jealously guarded hours when you are at your freshest are called for. It may not give some ministers the same buzz that they get from being always on the go attending to some pastoral crisis. But such preparation time is no mere luxury, ancillary to your work. It is at the very heart of your work.[3]

## The preacher as pastor

Preaching is one aspect only of pastoral relationship, but it is one of the most prominent. First impressions of their vicar's preaching will contribute a lot to a congregation's relationship with him or her. This does not mean, mercifully, that that relationship is fatally threatened if the opening sermons are muddled, inadvertently offensive or way over people's heads. As I reflect on my early preaching in a church where I was curate in charge, I seriously wonder whether and how it connected to people's lives in that particular rural community (I recall a rather detailed exposition of the doctrine of the Trinity from Acts 2 on my third Sunday), but I am the more grateful for the tolerance of the congregation that allowed a pastoral relationship to grow.

It is nevertheless important to recognize how your early preaching will set the tone for your ministry. A vicar whose sermons give the impression that (for all they care) the gospel has never been preached or known in a place before their arrival, or that they have all the answers to revival in that parish from their wealth and depth of previous experience, is hardly fostering a receptive atmosphere for the ministry of the word. Humility and good listening are essential prerequisites for preaching as for pastoral care generally, and the preacher embarking on a new sphere of ministry needs to balance a readiness to share what they have discovered of the riches of Christ with a readiness to understand the people with whom they are called to share it. Only so will *communication* happen, and *receptivity* to that message grow.

Serious work has been done on methods of 'exegeting' one's congregation (and community), seeking to understand in depth the ways they are formed by factors such as local culture, shared memory and ecclesiastical tradition.[4] This is vital if what we preach is to be shaped in such a way as to be heard. It is something in which to invest time and energy from the start of one's ministry in a place, and throughout it. One preacher recently wrote with excitement of practising the 'daily diary' scheme suggested by Roger Van Harn.[5] This involves enlisting a small group of volunteers from the congregation who will record, on a daily basis over one to four weeks, both one significant experience (positive or negative) and some 'words of faith or hope' which were important to them that day. These 'diaries' are then shared in confidence either alone with the preacher, or with the other diarists also present. Thus the preacher can stay in touch with actual (as opposed to merely imaginary) concerns of at least a few of the congregation at any one time.

It may be necessary to overcome some cultural resistance in yourself, and others, before such a process of 'listening to the listeners' is taken seriously. Especially, it should not be conveniently dismissed as a thinly veiled way of trimming down the gospel to the tastes of the hearers. It is, rather, a process by which the fog of misunderstanding that so often hangs between preacher and listener can be penetrated, and the gift and challenge of the gospel truly received. As I reflect on my years as a parish priest I now wonder whether two basic problems were profoundly connected. On the one hand, I did not sense that my preaching was particularly effective. On the other hand, I felt that in my pastoral visiting I was not 'sharing the gospel' on a personal level as I should. Could it have been the case that instead of feeling guilty about not always talking about matters of faith on pastoral visits, I should have embraced more gladly the opportunity afforded by these visits to learn in some depth the way the people and the community ticked? My sermons might then have connected to them better. In light of recent events and trends in the farming community, I think back with regret at my lack of any serious attempt to understand the agricultural practices and ways of life in my parish. Instead of seeing an interest in local history, geography and culture as a hobby, aside from the 'main business' of pastoral work, I would today see it as central to that business.

# The preacher as leader

For a minister in charge of a church, the roles of 'preacher' and 'leader' inevitably get intertwined in a variety of ways. The minister-leader not only preaches, but also has final responsibility for decisions about *whether* and *when* sermons are to take place, and *of what kind*, and *who* should preach them. He or she will often not be the sole 'preacher' or 'teacher' in a church, but will have the responsibility for the *organization* of the preaching and teaching that goes on there, in such a way as to make good use of the differing gifts of the various preachers and offer a varied, nourishing and coherent diet to congregations. This raises a number of issues.

## Occasions for preaching

A new vicar asked his colleagues whether the congregation at the 8 a.m. Holy Communion were used to having a sermon. The answer was no. 'Well, they're going to get one', was his response. The tone of the remark was combative, but the outcome was positive, because the sermons preached were brief and pungent homilies that fitted the mood and time of the service. They enriched the diet, and I suspect that most of the congregation learned not to mind waiting five minutes longer for their breakfast. Recently, in contrast, I have heard anecdotes of leisurely twenty-minute teaching sermons at early Communion services, sometimes accompanied by flipchart or OHP. Congregations can be amazingly longsuffering, but such a preaching strategy surely does not fit this kind of occasion; and preachers who (as it were) intrude upon an occasion with inappropriate preaching and a 'bull in a china shop' mentality are unlikely to win a hearing.

Sensitivity to tradition is important. My first year in one parish there was an excellent congregation for the Christmas carol service, with the village church full. The next year it was down by about a third. Why? I never enquired (though facing these things honestly seems to me now an excellent idea), but I wonder whether it was because on top of a full diet of carols and readings, I had preached a 15-minute sermon the previous year? There are plenty of sensitive ways of keeping a carol service fresh and meaningful, letting the readings and carols themselves tell the story, without prolonging it by inserting a sermon. But traditions vary. A neighbouring church was regularly packed out for a carol service with sermon. It is surprising how receptive people may be to a sermon when it is seen as being integral to the occasion.

## Proclamation and teaching

The vicar has the responsibility for seeing both that the good news is faithfully proclaimed and that disciples and would-be disciples are nurtured in faith. The difficulty for many Anglicans (and others) is that it often seems necessary to focus all efforts at nurturing in the one service that is, for many, the only 'church' gathering of the week. This main act of worship thus becomes the main occasion for *teaching*, especially where the church and/or minister is in the Evangelical tradition.

I find it helpful, however, to think of the role of preaching within the main weekly Eucharist as 'proclamation' rather than 'teaching'.[6] It is an opportunity to focus on some central aspect of the gospel, as seen in one or more of the day's readings. This serves both to confirm the faithful in their sense of identity and calling, and to make known the good news to those attending who are not yet part of the family of faith. Both God's gift announced in this gospel, and the human response to it, are then enacted in the sacrament of Holy Communion. Thus preaching truly becomes part of the worship, as well as concentrating on core truth at the time when the church is 'being the church' at its most public and explicit. It can also be planned so as to dovetail with other evangelistic activities such as Alpha.

Such a sermon is precisely appropriate to a congregation which *does* include many for whom this is the week's (increasingly, perhaps the month's) only church gathering. Such people may well be more receptive to a concise, fresh presentation of a central gospel theme than to extended in-depth examination of a passage, or of some doctrinal or ethical matter. There is no reason why such 'proclamation' should always be in monologue form. In some settings 'interactive' forms of preaching may enable a far deeper hearing of the word.[7] But you should not be hoodwinked by rumours of the sermon's demise[8] into thinking that a carefully crafted and delivered monologue is now unable to do an effective job of 'proclamation'.

Where then is the place for 'teaching', helping people explore Scripture in depth and wrestle in detail with applying faith to daily life? Although 'proclamation' can certainly include elements of teaching, I suggest that the main occasions for it might be Sunday evening services, midweek gatherings or (as often in the USA) adult 'Sunday schools' in parallel with children's groups either preceding or following the main Sunday morning service. An advantage of moving it out of the 'main' service is that it gives liberty for the full range of contemporary educational methods to be employed. In no other sphere today would an extended monologue be regarded as a sufficient and effective method for *teaching*. This requires a whole range of approaches. Input, lecture-style, is of course required (people don't learn and grow through the pooling of ignorance). But such input needs to be complemented by printed material, visual aids of one kind or another, opportunity for questions and discussion, and projects in which learners are active, not merely passive. Really worthwhile teaching benefits from being loosened from the inevitably formal constraints of a service of worship. In addition, it will be those who really want 'teaching' who will find it. This seems to be a dominical principle: Jesus told pithy parables to the crowds, and followed them up with longer discussions with those who were interested (Mark 4.1-20).

The vital thing is that the minister in charge should ensure that whoever is 'preaching' or 'teaching' on a particular occasion, the purpose of the occasion and the word-ministry within it is clearly understood.

## Visions and agenda

It is also important to distinguish between both 'proclamation' and 'teaching' on the one hand, and the leader's 'pep-talk' on the other. There is a natural tendency to blend the roles of preacher and motivator/administrator/chair, and this is not always helpful. The 'notices' start to mingle with the 'sermon' in subtle or not-so-subtle ways, and preaching becomes merely a vehicle for advancing an agenda.

A strong doctrine of the ministry of the word, and a strong sense of the representative character of what goes on in public worship, help to maintain this distinction. If you believe, as I do, that our calling as preachers (in both 'proclaiming' and 'teaching') is to feed the flock of God with the word of God,[9] you will be reluctant to contaminate the food with the additives of your own plans and ideas for the church. The place for those is at church council meetings and the like – and occasionally, as 'notices', in a service: not, I suggest, in the sermon or the 'teaching' programme.

As a conscientious preacher, you will rightly want to be relevant, and to help the congregation to see that biblical truth should make a difference to the way that a church operates. This is, indeed, a part of the point of 'exegeting the congregation', recommended above. Sharing a scripturally rooted vision for the church's life can be helpful and inspiring. The problem comes when you give the impression that *the* upshot of this particular passage, or doctrine, or whatever, is that *this* plan or idea (of yours) should be put into effect.[10] When a vicar draws from a text like Isaiah 43.19 – 'I am about to do a new thing' – the message that the church must go ahead and accept their plans (to which he or she has already persuaded a reluctant PCC) to remove the pews and re-order the church building, the discerning member of the flock is right to smell a rat. It is not just a matter of right handling of the Bible, vital though that is, but also of the way power is exercised. As vicar you are in a perilous position, all too able to take advantage of the respect traditionally afforded the occupant of a pulpit to seek to advance your own purposes. However high-minded those purposes may be, the flock is not fed when Scripture is simply suborned to promulgate them. Those in the 'charismatic' tradition may be especially vulnerable to an over-tight alignment of specific passages of Scripture and 'the way God is leading us', but it is a temptation to which preachers of all stripes can readily succumb.

### Co-ordinating a preaching team

It is enriching if those who preach are able to meet together regularly to reflect on their preaching ministry. Preachers *de facto* share in the leadership of the church, even if they hold no official post, and it is good in these contexts to air matters such as the relationship of the sermons to the overall direction of the church, discussed above. Practically, such meetings are opportunities to share preliminary ideas for sermons. The Revised Common Lectionary offers good opportunity for series of sermons, whether of the 'proclamation' or 'teaching' variety; clearly, if these are going to work, co-ordination among the preachers is essential.[11] But more than this, they are a chance to reflect together on the preaching that is past, and (where they have been able to hear one another) to offer honest but supportive mutual feedback. Here the leadership role, and vulnerability, of the incumbent are crucial.

## The preacher as human

Preaching is the occasion when you as minister are 'in role' in the most public way. Personalities vary in their degree of enjoyment of this public exposure. Some relish it, others dread it; between those extremes, many (like me) find it fulfilling yet draining. There is a requirement for a peculiar blend of vulnerability (if people cannot see that God's word has touched us, it is unlikely to touch them) and impersonality (people must recognize that God and his word are far greater than the signs they see in you). But if you believe in the grace of God mediated by his Spirit to those whom he calls to represent him and represent his people, you will also believe that God can use the full range of personalities in this representation. One of the most important things for a minister to bear in mind, looking ahead to a lifetime's preaching, is the symbiotic relationship between their growth as a person and their growth as a preacher.

Like many, I have found the Myers-Briggs Type Indicator (MBTI®) a very helpful tool for understanding personality and its impact on ministry and preaching. There are good resources for exploring this.[12] Here I simply suggest the value of exploring the 'shadow side', and of exercising the less-preferred functions of our personality. This does not mean that you seek to change 'who you are', but that you seek to become more rounded, as you strengthen your less-developed faculties.

This can make a significant difference to preaching. For example, as someone with a 'Sensing' preference, I have seldom had difficulty assembling plenty of material for a sermon. But I now see the potential of letting my 'Intuitive' faculty play a greater role in welding such material into a 'whole' that can be more readily received by a congregation than an agglomeration of details.

There are differing views on how much self-revelation is appropriate in preaching. On the one hand, if you do not reveal ways in which the gospel has had an impact on you, your message will fail to connect and convince. When I started as a preacher I wanted to hide behind good exegesis. I recall a turning-point when I decided to relate the story of the lost son (Luke 15.11-32) to my own much less colourful form of teenage rebellion. Immediately I sensed a new level of rapport with the congregation. On the other hand, preaching that revolves entirely around the preacher's own experiences detracts from the message. Not only does the preacher become the centre of attention, rather than Christ, but the experiences themselves, far from creating a bond with the congregation, may soon start to create a sense of alienation; for one person's life will appear to be as different from other people's as it is similar.

Emotional stunting and intellectual blinkers will show themselves in our preaching, whether you like it or not. There are of course other, deeper reasons, quite separate from preaching, why we should seek to grow through these things, but sheer self-respect (to say nothing of the desire to incarnate the word, even in some small way) should prevent you from ignoring their effect on your preaching. Conversely, however, your readiness to accommodate in your preaching new insights about yourself, the world, Scripture and God is a significant impetus to personal growth. Giving voice to an idea or perspective in public is, among other things, an act of personal commitment which, whatever it may do for the hearers, can enlarge your own life as you follow through the implications of what you have said. I remember the first time I referred in a sermon to the Jewish people as 'brothers and sisters'. This not only expressed a newly-expanded vision of the purposes of God, but furthered my desire to find ways of exercising (in life as well as in words) a true 'ministry of reconciliation'. Preaching is an exciting adventure, even if, like Paul, we constantly remember our insufficiency (2 Corinthians 2.16).

## Contact

The College of Preachers runs a range of training courses and conferences, and publishes a biannual journal. For more details visit www.collegeofpreachers.org.uk or contact The Administrator, College of Preachers, 14A North Street, Bourne, Lincolnshire PE10 9AB. Tel. 01778 422929.
email administrator@collegeofpreachers.org.uk

# Knowing whose service it is

Stephen Conway

Whether you are moving to a first incumbency or looking afresh at what you do a few years into the job, now is the time to explore in new ways the possibilities presented by your own experience of worship. This means that you are excited and nervous at the same time: both are good for generating an energetic humility. Of course, you want this your ministry to be identified by its confidence and vision; but acknowledging that we might be a bit nervous is fine, too, because it helps us to see more clearly that it is not all up to us, because God is down to it with us and for us.

While we worship at all times of day and night and on every day and in a great array of contexts, what unites all worship is that it is divine: it is of God, for God, to God and always in Christ and through the Holy Spirit. God is not only the object of our worship but the author of it, too. This may seem obvious to you and to me; but this does not excuse us from the need for constant reminder.

The incumbent may be the resident expert on liturgical form and practice, but that is a consequence not a justification for his or her role as the authoritative gatherer of God's people around the altar of gladness.

This does not mean that you come into a new community ready to be a doormat. The minister is given real and powerfully symbolic authority in the worship of the Church. You have been set aside by the grace of God and the choice of the Church to represent in your leading and guiding of worship the objective breaking-in of our transcendent and immanent God into our world and our lives. However we have come into their midst, our calling is an embodied reminder to any congregation that we are not going through the rituals of a self-regarding club but doing something both wonderful and dangerous: doing what human beings do best, even at their worst, which is to offer their sacrifice of praise in response to the perfect sacrifice of God's self in Jesus Christ and to serve the consequences of that sacrifice as agents of reconciliation and new life in God's growing kingdom.

## Paying attention

When I was first ordained, I encountered an elderly lady in the parish who greeted me with a big hug and told me that she had known 42 curates in the parish and a 43rd wouldn't do her any harm. Clergy are very often told by churchwardens, 'Vicars come and go, but we stay.' Since most new vicars are coming from outside the parish, there is a heaven-sent opportunity to listen to the rhythms of the community and how they are already being expressed in the worship of the Church. For instance, a town centre church I know has a Commercial Harvest each year which makes real sense in reflecting the fruits of the retailers by whose operations the Church is surrounded. A sentimental vicar with a passion for marrows and onions is not going to reflect that community which feels that the church is listening to local rhythms. If you begin with developing this aptitude for listening it will become habitual and remain a key part of your quality assurance in worship all the time you minister in that place.

The same applies to inhabiting the patterns of service we find when we arrive in a new place. As a student I had occasionally attended *Book of Common Prayer* services, mostly for the music associated with them. Where I served in two curacies the *BCP* was no longer used. Whether the *BCP* or another form of service, you may well encounter a pattern of worship which is unfamiliar. Before you give any serious thought to changing the pattern, first inhabit it. Be sensitive to the cadence of the language and to customary liturgical posture and gesture. Don't be too proud to talk to a neighbouring priest who is established in those rhythms and see how she does it.

An important part of paying attention is being alert to the personality and character of the various congregations in your care. People have mixed reactions to personality typing processes like Myers-Briggs and the Enneagram. I commend both as ways in which to understand our own priorities and needs and to identify better the dynamics of a community. Myers-Briggs has identified, for instance, that the clergy are much more likely to be introvert than people in the congregation. This has implications for a range of possibilities, from the reaction to moving the lectern three inches to approaches to silence in worship.

It is also observable that particular churches express a dominant personality type in the way in which they worship, welcome newcomers and reach out to the community. This is not to make a judgement about which is better; but it is wise to observe what that style is and in what ways your presence alters it or interacts with it. When I was training to be a teacher, I was told by a wise guide that noisy teachers make noisy classrooms.

## Keeping recollected

One of the principal reasons why people stay away from church is not that they do not believe in God, but because their limited experience of worship is that we Christians do not really care about it. This begins with us. There is, sadly, too much evidence around of clergy who have stopped praying, who treat worship as a necessary routine, who have become functional atheists. It is very important, therefore, that you pay attention from the start both to how your own spiritual life and discipline contributes to the regular worship of the church and to how you hope that the worship will continue to feed you. I strongly recommend that all of us, therefore, make a *rule of life* – which is regularly reviewed with a trusted guide – which sees the worship of the church as an integral part of our own spiritual diet and not separate from it; and which incorporates a review of our attitudes and approaches to worship into our regular self-examination. When people tell us as they leave church what a nice service it has been, we know that they can mean anything, including the opposite of what they have said. It is a major spiritual responsibility for us to be alert to our own drifting away from the heart of what it is to be a worshipping servant.

On a daily basis, the best litmus test for us is attending to how attentive we are being to the Spirit of God when we are officiating at services. By this I do not just mean that we are professionally prepared and know what is supposed to be happening. What I am really getting at is how far we have prepared in prayer and are waiting on God beforehand, so that we are recollected in the presence of God and that we have made the worship our key priority for that time. This will be demonstrated not only in the quality of our preaching, but also in our singing, in the pace of the service and in our confidence in leading the congregation into unselfconscious silence.

This is not just or even primarily important for our own sake. We fulfil our role in worship partly by creating space in which others will be met by God and by setting an example of expectant attentiveness which gives people confidence that this might really happen to them. More than that, the people of the parish need to be assured that you as their parish priest are bearing them on your loving heart to God in the public worship of the church as well as in your private prayers.

## Building a team

Quite rightly, the Church no longer refers in its liturgical rubrics to the 'celebrant' but to the 'president' or 'presider'. This is not a trivial change. The use of 'celebrant' harks back to a hieratic understanding of ministry which makes the minister the only actor in the performance of worship and consigns the congregation to the role of audience. The truth is that the worship is offered and celebrated by the whole people of God. There is an important sense in which the minister is the God-given conductor of the orchestra, but the music is the product of a collaborative and multi-layered pattern of passion, skill, practice and attentiveness which is the sum of many parts. The minister presides over worship with the humility of Christ as described in Philippians 2 and as Christ himself acts in the washing of the disciples' feet in John 13. Worship is what human beings are made for, and you, the minister, are a product, servant and primarily beneficiary of the worship offered by the whole Church.

> **A curate was presiding at the Eucharist for the first time after having been ordained to the ministerial priesthood. The church was full of people, both the regular congregation and his family, friends and others who had supported his formation so far for this ministry. When it came to the breaking of the bread, he broke the bread rather clumsily. His vicar, supposedly supporting him on his immediate right, leaned over and hissed at him, 'Now you have spoiled my whole service.' We need no commentary on this statement other than to be reminded that the worship does not belong to the clergy like some kind of fiefdom.**

Discerning and encouraging the gifts which people bring to worship is an absolutely vital part of your role. Sharing pastoral ministry is not sufficient in itself. You need to bear witness to shared ministry in the way you lead worship.

Encouraging other to participate reflects the humility of God in emptying the space which enabled creation to be. Part of the vicar's creative task is to make way for others with the gifts to devise liturgies for children or special occasions, to lead prayers and to preach. Of course, this does not diminish the vicar's responsibility to seek to guarantee that God and God's people are always given the best all can offer; and that you are there to lead and embody the agreed vision of the parish. It is no good if a particular intercessor does a Jules Verne and takes us all round the world, or seeks to correct the sermon. Think of the times that you may have been asked to help devise a special liturgy with young people where it has been too full of good things. It is a proper exercise of your authority to advise and correct; but only if you are offering encouragement and training, too.

You may already be working with a worship team or may encounter one in the parish when you arrive. They may be anxious and defensive at any time because they have come to invest a great deal in their role, encouraged in a certain style by you or your predecessor. They may be waiting for you to relieve them of a burden which they have longed to surrender; they may be hoping that former constraints will be lifted by the greater freedom you are prepared to offer; or they may be expecting you to close them down. As with everything else, wait, listen and love. Do not be afraid to allow your own gifts of prayer, theology, experience and personality to have an impact. Your integrity is vital. At the same time, God has put these people in this place to celebrate their gifts. Honour this – even when it would be easier to do the jobs yourself or you would like them to adapt quickly to the changes which you can now see are necessary. It is a fine balance to strike between celebrating beautiful and inspiring liturgies where you cannot see the join and allowing people to make mistakes that may be inspiring in themselves.

## Being an agent of orderly change

It is a growing and happy trend for people to prefix whatever description they offer of their defining tradition with 'open'. It is increasingly common for open evangelical clergy to be invited to become vicar of parishes which have a catholic tradition of worship and spirituality. You may be in this position yourself. Trying to understand another tradition from the inside is a further refinement of the management of change that you will inevitably face. If you are coming to a parish new do not accept the post if your only object would be to change everything at once. If you have been in post a while, review those changes for which you have been directly responsible. It is so important to strike a true balance between your own beliefs and experience and the heartfelt traditions of the parish.

When I went to be a parish priest, I had determined ideas about the conduct of the Good Friday liturgy. I made inaccurate assumptions about what had gone before and did not carry the congregation with me. I had an important lesson to learn about co-operation and listening to the mood. My chastened approach the following year which invited people to find their own place in a more relaxed and inclusive liturgy had startling effects: people participated much more fully than I could possibly have sought to engineer. So honour and cherish the good in what you discover, often to your own surprise. Assume unless proven wrong that you will encounter holiness and grace. Investigate the genuine theology behind the use or the absence of particular vestments, liturgical actions and sacramental devotions. Do not be frightened of them. Seek advice from clergy of that tradition about what the essence of it is, rather than the fringe issues about which people can be prejudiced from the outside and obsessed within. Discern the pastoral needs which the existing liturgies support.

Wherever you are, familiarize yourself with the worship-related Canons of the Church of England so that you know what parameters you are working within. As with the rubrics of *Common Worship*, you may discover that the options and resources for lively worship which is both profound and evangelistic are wider than you thought.

You are in holy orders. Order of some kind is necessary in worship so that, at the very least, people are protected from harm. As a parish priest, you are a servant of God's creative order in the developing spiritual life of the community. That order does not always mean formality, but sometimes it will. The ordering is not just of the worship itself but of the building, so that the space sets free the worship which expresses the vision of the congregation. It is a good ordering of the words people need in front of them, preferably without a plethora of books and with technology which works. It is the ordering by the power of the Holy Spirit of the Body of Christ, becoming what we eat in the Eucharist.

## Being heavenly minded

We are only any earthly use if we are heavenly minded. The test of the worship in our parishes is whether it offers a foretaste of the heavenly banquet as something more than a theological abstraction. Would you be there if you didn't have to be? As a missionary church, would you yet want to invite new people along? These are questions we all face as incumbents: it's all right to ask.

# Appendix I

# The short guide to some things they may not have told you

David Ison

## Difficult people

There are difficult people in every church. It is absolutely normal. That is one reason why the Church exists – to be somewhere that all can be welcomed in the name of the hospitality of Christ. People who find it difficult to be accepted are attracted to a place where they are welcomed. And we can all be difficult.

But what do you do when someone's behaviour, personal habits or criminal propensities threaten to disrupt the life and worship of the church and its ministry? The main principle is just the same as dealing with any corporate behaviour difficulty: agree and maintain boundaries. These will need to be flexible: one of the gifts brought by people who don't fit in is that they make us reassess what's really important about what we do. But while we seek to love them appropriately, difficult people have no right to hurt, oppress or abuse others. The best positive strategy is to find a way of their needs being catered for which minimizes disruption to other people: for example, to allow a paedophile to come to evening service where children are not present, or to encourage a disruptive child to come to a family service rather than a solemn Eucharist. If the person has a hysterical or narcissistic personality, it can be very helpful to give them a regular time (fortnightly or monthly, perhaps) when they have someone's undivided attention for an hour, and then to say 'no' politely but firmly to blandishments, manipulation or threats designed to get attention at other times.

It is important to see working with those who are demanding as something which is the corporate task of the church, and not the sole responsibility of the minister or the person that the difficult character has latched on to. How often does the local church review its care for difficult people, including those who will simply turn up on the minister's doorstep or at the back of church? Does the PCC or leadership group look for ways of meeting the needs of all? Having a church food cupboard and never giving money are two good places to start.

An individual minister shouldn't get trapped or manipulated into thinking they have to meet the presenting needs of everyone; although people will try to force us to feel guilty, it's a game that we should always opt out of. The question 'What *can* we do to help you grow closer to God?' may start with the priority of material needs, but will lead each person towards the encounter with Christ which alone can meet their deepest needs.

## Difficult churches

Every church has its skeletons in the cupboard, which gradually emerge in the first few years of a new parish priest's ministry. They also have people who use the church to meet their own needs. But some churches have an inherited culture which has in one way or another resulted in the church being 'captured' by a group of people who are working out their own pathologies through the way the church is, and whose personal identities are bound up with the way they have made it. Addictive or chaotic personalities, for example, may depend on a rigid structure of belief and practice, whether of evangelical fervour or high-church daily mass, to provide some stability in their lives. People who feel powerless may relish the opportunity to control parts of the church's life, even if they have no vision for how it should be other than keeping it as it is. Small communities may replicate the power structures of local society in the ordering of church life, and feel threatened if this is questioned.

In such churches, ministers need to become aware of the hidden agendas, and tread the tightrope between alienating and humiliating those in control, who need spiritual growth and encouragement, and allowing them to subvert the mission of the gospel by keeping the church as a means of meeting their needs rather than including the needs of others. An external consultant or supervisor can be invaluable in helping clergy understand and work with such difficult situations.

## Feeling guilty about visiting

Most ministers feel guilty because they don't visit enough. Part of this is inevitably due to the 'George Herbert' syndrome, where the aspiration is to visit the whole parish regularly, forgetting that Herbert had 300 souls to look after with the help of a curate or two, whereas modern clergy have thousands, as well as administrative requirements (many rooted in legislation) which Herbert didn't dream of. But it's also difficult to keep up the visiting of those in the congregation in regular need, let alone those who don't have obvious problems. Living with this guilt is inevitable: but part of its resolution lies in how ministers set priorities. What visiting is important, and why? How can the church develop mutual support and pastoral care, so that the minister uses her or his time most effectively with those in need? A basic system of pastoral care exercised by church members can enable the minister to concentrate on urgent, difficult and mission situations. And a little visiting regularly does more for morale than binge visiting every so often. I have found visiting people outside the church invaluable for boosting morale and keeping the trials of church life in perspective.

Some ministers however feel guilty because they don't seem to achieve important things when they visit. Having another cup of tea with Mrs Jones seems an ineffective use of valuable time. This is where getting work priorities straight can really help. Who can help Mrs Jones, and how? It may be that our time is the most valuable gift we have to give her, and it speaks to her of God's love far more than any words we say. Whether you're visiting someone for the first time or the fifty-first, be open, as C. S. Lewis put it, to the adventure that [Christ] sends us, meeting someone at their point of need: for prayer, healing, or loving attentiveness.

## Household and parish

Once someone is ordained, they lose some of their privacy: they become, to some extent, a public person. For a vicar or minister in charge there is the added dimension of being the representative and focus of a particular group or groups of people, for whom the personality and life of the minister may be one of the few things they have in common that they're willing to talk about – and they will! Your private life will be a matter of interest to others, and a potential source of encouragement or scandal. Trying to guard it too closely will be taken as a sign of rejection, or that there's something to be hidden. But everyone needs privacy too. Married clergy's spouses and children can find that their partner, mother or father has got them into a limelight that can have very positive aspects, but which may be experienced as unwelcome or even destructive. Getting the balance right will vary according to situation and personalities involved. Good communication, honesty, and time spent on maintaining private life in some way, are essential. And sometimes the very curious will need tactfully reminding that the minister's home life is not the set of the parish soap opera. The use of a tied house for ministry is part of the question of privacy and a cause for careful negotiation between the needs and expectations of the parish and the minister's own household needs.

When ministers are public people, their actions – and those of their spouses – can be marked in public too. If ministry takes place in a large and relatively anonymous city, then this is less of an issue. But for those in a town or village, meeting people in shops or restaurants is quite likely: and for those looking for a quiet romantic dinner or to buy something special, this can be off-putting. If you want to be private, be ready to travel, or politely to rebuff or postpone pastoral encounters. It can be very irksome for a spouse to be promised some quality time and then see it hijacked by an immediate encounter with someone.

The question of having particular friends in the church or parish is usually addressed in training or title parish. But what happens when it's the vicar's – or spouse's – fortieth or sixtieth birthday, or a child's eighteenth? Is this a private or parish event? How private are family celebrations, and what is the local culture about inviting people round and celebrating personal and family milestones? Who should be included, and on what basis? And when leaving a parish: what names go on the Christmas card list, and for how long? How far is it appropriate to go back and visit people as friends, rather than the church as ex-vicar? The question of letting go and moving on is a delicate one.

## Feeling at home

Nearly all clergy live in tied accommodation. This can be difficult both for those who give up their own house, and for those who have never had one. The sense of powerlessness can begin at the start of a new post when the taste and needs of the new household don't fit with either what has gone before or the judgement of the Archdeacon, or the budget of the Parsonages Board. Having to live with things you haven't chosen, for the sake of the job, the inability to make major changes, the feeling of not being quite at home in a house which the minister doesn't own and will have to leave – all can take their toll on the feeling – or not – of being at home in a place.

As clergy progress through ministry, there is also the question of where 'home' actually is. In our mobile society this is less marked than it was, because it's a feeling that many people share: but it can be hard to be intimately involved in the affairs of a community one month and then no longer part of it the next, especially at the point of retirement – when the issue of where 'home' is to be takes on a much bigger dimension. Having to move home in order to change job can be a source of tension, and needs facing honestly, especially if it affects spouse and children adversely.

## Clergy spouses

Being a minister may at times be a sacrificial calling, but sacrificing spouse and family is not supposed to be on the agenda. It can be hard at times, however, for spouses to feel that they are as valued as the people alongside whom their partner ministers, however committed they themselves are to what the minister does. Having a way of being pastorally cared for by someone other than the vicar to whom they're married is one way of maintaining some spiritual health and balance. Another way is having a means of developing their own chosen 'career'. Some spouses devote themselves to child-rearing, and find this and their support of their spouse's ministry to be a fulfilling life-long role. Others begin in this mould, but then find God calling them to develop their own role, in church-based ministry or outside it: this can appear to upset the basis on which the relationship has been set up, and needs to be worked out carefully so that the minister finds ways of being supportive rather than feeling threatened.

A couple who see their ministry as joint, but with one partner being trained and licensed and the other not, may have to negotiate with their church as well as each other in order to avoid misunderstanding, for example about their roles in relation to other church staff members. There is also a scenario in which a frustrated spouse tries to work out their own vocation by exerting influence over the minister, which is an unhealthy situation needing resolution by enabling the spouse to find their own sphere of ministry. There may also be some differences between spouses who marry into ministry, and those whose partners were called into ordination after marriage; but spouses in either category may feel either that they have not necessarily chosen the lifestyle they lead, or that it is a positive improvement on available alternatives.

How the parish views the couple in the vicarage also varies. People may have a tradition of seeing the vicar's spouse as an unpaid curate, or of expecting nothing from them; or in some instances that they can 'get at' the minister by gaining influence over their spouse. If there is a tradition of ignoring the spouse, the reverse can also be true: spouses can feel frustrated at being on the outside, especially when seeing the minister struggling with parish issues, and try to get at the parish through the minister. And what happens if there are marital or family tensions and problems which other people pick up, or in which the parish becomes implicated? The importance of communication and negotiation is paramount in handling difficult boundaries between public role and necessary privacy.

## Vicarage children

In some churches there is the real bonus of a ready-made extended family, with good-hearted and competent child-minders and friends at the same stage of childhood on tap. In other churches the vicar's children may be the only ones in the Sunday school, the congregation may be taken up with their own (grand)children or out at work, and there may even be a few people who are obsessive about the minister's family life and their place in it and from whom a family need safeguarding. Clergy need to think about what is truly in the best interests of their children: living on the job entails compromises, not capitulation. Allowing children to go to another church with a youth group, or even not to church at all, may feel difficult, but honestly faced and explained it need not be. It can also be hard when socially exclusive local schools or particular educational needs indicate schooling away from the parish: but taking a stand on high-minded principle, as some clergy have done in the past, is not a substitute for loving concern for the real needs of each child. If the gospel isn't good news for clergy children, how can it be so for anyone? As they grow up children need more privacy than adults, and this needs sensitive handling, rather than, for example, assuming that a child's exploits will make good sermon illustration material. And there can sometimes be a real stigma to being a vicarage child in a parish or school, in which case children will need particular support and understanding.

## How to go on holiday

Some clergy hardly ever go on holiday. They can't face the effort of finding holiday cover for services (or of cancelling them) and of dealing with funerals and other issues that may arise; some may be reluctant to leave a vicarage unattended in an insecure area. It can be a surprise for former curates and assistant ministers to realize that they, not someone else, have the responsibility for arranging cover. How do you do it?

If there isn't a local (usually retired) priest willing to do holiday cover, it can be worth teaming up with a local colleague to cover one another's funerals and emergencies while going on holiday at different times. Readers are often willing to lead non-eucharistic services: it is usually easier to find clergy to lead evening communion services and have morning family services if morning cover for the Eucharist is not available; or even consult with the bishop about cancelling services if no one can be found. Time for holiday is essential to maintain spiritual life and the ability to minister effectively. Tell funeral directors whom to contact and when; don't leave the answerphone on and come back to a pile of messages, or check it while away (which means not having proper holiday time). And never leave an answerphone message that says or implies that the occupants of the vicarage are away – simply that they are off duty at this time. If security is a major issue, see if someone would be willing to live in while the occupants are away. In some areas, clergy may even have to load up the car in the garage and drive away round the back roads under cover of darkness in order to maintain security.

## Money

For many years vicars have been responsible for the collection of and accounting for parochial fees; although this may be devolved, responsibility remains with the parish priest. Being aware of how to do this, and also of the need for financial planning in the church, including budget planning and monitoring, accounts and balance sheets, are basic skills for parish clergy which may not have been dealt with in previous training. A good church treasurer is a great asset: if a treasurer is inexperienced, diocesan offices and other more local colleagues can generally offer advice and support. The Archbishops' Council's guide on payment of expenses (available from Ministry Division, Church House, Great Smith Street, London SW1P 3NZ) may be useful when there is a lack of clarity about what can be claimed: it is important for clergy to be seen to be objective about the handling of money, and not to misuse their position to gain financial advantage in the payment of fees and expenses, even if the parish encourages them to do so.

With regard to personal finance: many dioceses now organize occasional courses on financial planning, relating to matters such as income tax, investments and long-term planning, pensions and housing. Clergy with a stipend, no other income and a family to support have little room for financial manoeuvre, but there are charities available to help with particular needs: archdeacons or other church authorities can usually advise on these, and some dioceses operate a discretionary funding scheme. It can be tempting to slip into debt in order to fund one-off items; but any level of persistent debt, especially on credit cards, needs tackling as soon as possible before it gets out of control, and help should also be available for this.

## Getting help

The sooner problems are faced, the easier it will be to sort them out, whether they are financial, moral, emotional or physical, the minister's own problems or those of spouse and family. All churches have structures of some kind for dealing with difficult and delicate issues among ministers. Most now have confidential counselling available to help ministers and their families, which is separate from structures of management. Many too have sources of financial help for clergy in difficulties, sometimes administered confidentially through the archdeacon. It can also be possible to access help through GPs or generic counselling services if desired.

There can be a particular problem for spouses who are aware of problems their partner is having but are afraid of damaging the minister's situation if they ask for the help which their partner is unwilling or unable to seek. There is no easy answer to this: but a spouse has every right to find help to deal with the situation in which they find themselves, and to use confidential services in order to do so.

Don't be afraid to ask for help. Pride conspires with problems to create disasters. The ability to ask for help is a sign of maturity, not weakness.

# Useful contacts for further sources of support

There are several sources of help available to clergy who wish to review
concerns in their ministry or some personal issue with an independent person.

## Self-assisted assessment schemes or consultants' reviews

A number of dioceses have schemes whereby a member of the clergy can meet
with a trained volunteer to discuss matters of concern or reflect on his or her
ministry. Details will be available in the diocesan office or on the web site.

## Advisers in pastoral care and counselling

Nearly all dioceses have advisers in pastoral care and counselling. The advisers
will be qualified counsellors or psychotherapists available for consultation by
clergy. Names may be available in the *Church of England Yearbook* or in the
diocesan handbook or web site. In case of difficulty, an enquiry could be made
to the Secretary of the Anglican Association of Pastoral Care and Counselling,
Julie Barrett on 01392 258198.

## Society of Mary and Martha

This is an independent ecumenical charity providing support for people in
Christian ministry and/or their spouses at times of stress, crisis or burnout.
There is a regular programme of retreats, reading weeks and '12,000 mile
service' week; Tel: 01647 252752.

# Appendix 2

# Useful web sites

Roger Morris

If there was one piece of advice that deserved to be written in bold print on every page of this book then it is 'don't neglect the visiting' – there is no substitute for spending time with people, especially when it comes to deepening your awareness of the community in which you are based. However, the Internet is undoubtedly a rich source of information for today's busy minister. With that in mind, I have selected some of the most useful sites.

## Knowhere.co.uk

One of the most telling pieces of information one can glean from a tour of the parish is where people tend to meet. Young people may choose to congregate at the local bus shelter, some may hang out at the local sports and social club whereas others may get up to all kinds of things in the local cemetery. These places have been given the term 'hook-up spots' and they are defined by the web site www.knowhere.co.uk as that 'hallowed spot where everyone hangs around with their mates dreaming of the time when they can get into the pubs or clubs – a bench, a corner: you name it.'

The Knowhere Guide started out as a list of places to skateboard in the UK. It is a compilation of (unedited) information and views supplied by users of the Internet. It now gives the low down on pubs, cafés, coffee shops, restaurants, gigs, festivals, clubs, music venues, cinemas, playing fields and sports centres. All the information is submitted by Internet users so its accuracy cannot be guaranteed. However, the kind of information it provides cannot normally be obtained elsewhere.

## The 2001 Census

All the data from the 2001 census is available on the Internet but you do have to know how to access it. The key site is www.neighbourhood.statistics.gov.uk. Once you have accessed the site, you can then view the census data for the ward in which you live or, by changing your selection, you can view the data for your civic parish. However, the most accurate approach is to view the data by 'output area'. Many parishes consist of a number of output areas. To find the output area in question, you need to click on a link entitled 'interactive map' (which can take a while to download). A map of England and Wales will appear on the left and there will be a box on the right entitled 'Area selection'. This latter box should read '2003 Administrative Areas – National to Ward level' and will feature a 'change' button. If you click on the 'change' button then, from a list entitled 'available hierarchies', you can select '2003 Administrative Areas – National to Output Area Level' for the region in which you live. Once you have clicked on the 'apply' button then the box will change to include output areas. If you then insert a postcode above the map and click on 'find' then a map will appear of the area in which you are interested and, printed on the map, will be a code (e.g. 44UEHH0005). This code is the code for the output area. You can then move around the map in order to select all the output area codes for the area in which you are interested. If you have selected your output areas then you can click on the button entitled 'choose dataset' and return to main 'Neighbourhood Statistics' window which will now feature a window entitled 'Subjects for Selected Areas'. You will now be able to obtain detailed information on every subject covered by the census.

## Up My Street

The website www.upmystreet.com has long been a useful tool for house-buyers looking to research the neighbourhood into which they might be moving. A simple search by postcode produces a wealth of information about local schools, crime statistics, the performance of the local council and even a five day weather forecast. However, the most interesting piece of information is something called the ACORN profile. ACORN stands for 'A Classification of Residential Neighbourhoods'. The whole of the United Kingdom is classified by post code into 5 categories (based on affluence) that are broken down into 17 distinct groups that are, in turn, made up of 56 'typical' ACORN neighbourhood categories. The ACORN profile gives the best fit profile for the postcode you enter. ACORN profiles are drawn up by an organization called CACI (www.caci.co.uk) who describe themselves as 'the UK's leading consumer and market analysis company'. CACI draw their information from the 2001 Census as well as various market research and lifestyle databases and their profiles are then updated on an annual basis. CACI's own site also allows you to perform a postcode search once you have registered (which is free) and then logged on. The CACI site will also allow you to then probe the ACORN profile in order to discover detailed information about any particular neighbourhood category. Among the most useful pieces of information one can obtain are details about working habits, leisure interests, which newspapers are most commonly read and what food and drink people living in that post code might consume. All the details are provisional and will certainly not apply to everyone living in a particular postcode but the information obtained can act as a very good guide to what one is likely to find.

# Notes

## Chapter 1  The changing role of the vicar

1   A major review of clergy terms of service is currently in process.

2   See *Review of Clergy Terms of Service: Report on the first phase of the work* (GS 1527), Church House Publishing, 2004.

## Chapter 2  Continuing training

1   J. H. Newman, *An Essay on the Development of Christian Doctrine*, 1909, 1.1.7.

2   The Archbishops' Council, *Mind the Gap: Integrated Continuing Ministerial Education for the Church's Ministers*, Church House Publishing, 2001, p. 29.

3   *Mind the Gap*, p. 62.

4   *Mind the Gap*, p. 50.

## Chapter 3  Self-management

1   There are signs that this is changing. Section 4 of the influential *Affirmation and Accountability – practical suggestions for preventing clergy stress, sickness and ill health in retirement* (Society of Mary and Martha, 2002; www.sheldon.uk.com) report offers a series of important recommendations for the reforming of traditional practice.

2   William Bridger points out the important difference between 'change' and 'transition'. Change is external – new home, new job, new job description. Transition is the internal, psychological adjustment we must make if we are successfully to adapt to the change. 'It isn't the changes that do you in, it's the transitions', *Managing Transitions – making the most of change*, Da Capo Press, 2003, p. 1.

3   David Maitland, *Looking Both Ways – A theology for mid-life*, John Knox Press, 1985, pp. 1–17.

4   I have explored this theme in more depth in *Choice, Desire and the Will of God – What more do you want?*, SPCK, 2002.

5   I have adapted this from an even more provocative thought attributed to Laurens van der Post: 'The greatest influence upon us is the life our parents have *not* had.'

6   The title of an important study by the Mary and Martha Society. See note 1 above.

7   Sarah Savage in *Beholding the Glory*, ed. Jeremy Begbie, Darton, Longman & Todd, 2001, p. 66.

8   *The Good Listener – Helen Bamber, a life against cruelty*, Weidenfeld & Nicolson, 1998, p. 135.

9   Most dioceses in the Church of England provide free, confidential counselling (usually six sessions initially) for clergy who need particular help and support.

## Chapter 4 Spiritual life

1    Francis Dewar, *Called or Collared*, SPCK, 1991, 2000.

2    John A. Sanford, *Ministry Burnout*, Westminster John Knox Press, 1992; Mary Anne Coates, *Clergy Stress*, SPCK, 1989.

3    *Alternative Service Book* copyright © The Central Board of Finance of the Church of England, 1980, The Archbishops' Council, 1999.

4    Chester P. Michael and Marie C. Norrisey, *Prayer and Temperament*, The Open Door Inc. 1984, 1991.

5    Harold Miller, *Finding a Personal Rule of Life*, Grove Spirituality Series, 1987, 2003.

6    E.g., *Celebrating the Saints*, Canterbury Press, 1998.

7    Rule of the Society of St John the Evangelist.

8    *Retreats* magazine available from The Retreat Association, the Central Hall, 256 Bermondsey Street, London SE1 3UJ or Christian bookshops.

9    *Rule for a New Brother*, Foreword by Henri J. M. Nouwen, Darton, Longman & Todd, 1973, 1986.

10   There are many books on Spiritual Direction but Anne Long, *Approaches to Spiritual Direction*, Grove Spirituality Series, third edition 1998, remains a very good introduction. Kenneth Leach, *Soul Friend*, Darton, Longman & Todd, 1994 is a classic. One of my personal favourites is Margaret Guenther, *Holy Listening: the Art of Spiritual Direction*, Darton, Longman & Todd, 1992.

11   www.24/7prayer.com

12   C.S. Lewis, *The Screwtape Letters*, Fount, 1998.

## Chapter 5 Direction: discerning and communicating vision

1    John Adair and John Nelson (eds), *Creative Church Leadership*, Canterbury Press, 2004, p. 7.

2    Andrew J. DuBrin, *The Complete Idiot's Guide to Leadership*, Alpha Books, Macmillan, second edition, 2000, quoted in Steven Croft, *Transforming Communities, Re-imagining the Local Church for the 21st Century*, Darton, Longman & Todd, 2002, p. 35.

3    See Russ Parker, *Forgiveness is Healing*, Darton, Longman & Todd, 1993, for its 'Christian Day of Atonement Service', pp. 162–7.

4    George Barna, *The Power of Vision*, Regal Books, 1992, p. 98.

5    Quoted by M. Fullan, *The New Meaning of Educational Change*, Cassell, 1991, p. 31.

6    Tom Marshall, *Understanding Leadership*, Sovereign World, 1991, p. 212.

## Chapter 6  Mission

1    Christian Schwarz, *Natural Church Development*, Churchsmart Resources, 1996.

2    See Paul McPartlan, *The Eucharist Makes the Church: Henri de Lubac and John Zizioulas in dialogue*, T&T Clark, 1993.

3    See Edward Dowler and Brendan Clover, *An Everlasting Gift*, Tufton Books, 2004.

4    *On the Way: Church of England schools in the new millennium*, Church House Publishing, 2000.

5    *Mission-shaped Church*, Church House Publishing, 2004.

6    Useful publications for further reflection include: J. Finney, *Finding Faith Today: How does it Happen?*, Swindon: Bible Society, 1992; M. Green, *Evangelism through the Local Church*, Hodder & Stoughton, 1993; B. Jackson, *Hope for the Church*, Church House Publishing, 2002; Morisy, *Beyond the Good Samaritan*, Mowbray, 1997; M. Moynagh, *Changing World, Changing Church*, Monarch, 2001; R. Warren, *Being Human, Being Church*, HarperCollins, 1991; R. Warren, *The Healthy Churches' Handbook*, Church House Publishing, 2004.

7    For a helpful overview and analysis of nurture courses see M. Booker and M. Ireland, *Evangelism – which way now?*, Church House Publishing, 2004.

8    John V. Taylor, *The Go-Between God*, SCM Press, 1973.

9    The five marks of mission are: To proclaim the Good News of the kingdom; to teach, baptize and nurture new believers; to respond to human need by loving service; to seek to transform unjust structures of society; to strive to safeguard the integrity of creation and sustain and renew the life of the earth.

10    Douglas Coupland, *Girlfriend in a Coma*, HarperCollins, 1998.


## Chapter 7  Parish systems

1    The Shaftesbury Society, 16 Kingston Road, London SW19 1JZ; Tel: 020 8239 5555; www.shaftesburysociety.org

2    Stephen Covey, *The Seven Habits of Highly Effective People*, Free Press, 1990.


## Chapter 8  Leadership and teamwork

1    For details of the research and how to apply it, see R. Meredith Belbin, *Management Teams – Why they succeed or fail*, Heinemann, 1981; R. Meredith Belbin, *Team Roles and Work*, Butterworth-Heinemann, 1993.

2    Get in touch with your local CME advisers for more information on this.

3    Chris Edmondson, *Fit to Lead*, Darton, Longman & Todd, 2002, p. 109.

## Chapter 9 Context

1    The Rule of St Benedict, Chapter 3.

2    *Faith in the City*, Church House Publishing, 1985.

3    The Arthur Rank Centre, Stoneleigh Park, Warwickshire  CV8 2LZ; Rural Theology Association (www.rural-theology.org.uk); Farming Information for Rural Ministry – email bulletins from alan.spedding@btopenworld.com (An Arthur Rank Centre project partly financed by DEFRA's Rural Support Initiative Fund.)

4    Andrew Bowden, *Ministry in the Countryside*, Mowbray, 1994, p. 47.

5    See Bob Jackson, *Hope for the Church*, Church House Publishing, 2002; Robert Warren, *Being Human, Being Church*, Marshall Pickering, 1995; Robert Warren and Bob Jackson, *There are Answers,* Springboard, 2002; Robert Warren, *The Healthy Churches' Handbook,* Church House Publishing, 2004. As of October 2004, Springboard has been succeeded by Fresh Expressions [www.freshexpressions.org.uk].

6    John Clarke, 'The Ministry of the Rural Church', lecture given at the Arthur Rank Centre, Stoneleigh, 5 November 1996.

7    Ron Wood, 'No priest? What your church lacks is an LWL', *Church Times,* 14 January 2002.

8    The Leveson Centre for the Study of Ageing, Spirituality and Social Policy, Temple House, Fen End Road, Temple Balsall, Knowle, Solihull B93 0AN.

## Chapter 10 Public ministry

1    On this see especially Neville Clark, *Preaching in Context: Word, worship and the people of God*, Kevin Mayhew, 1991.

2    Thomas G. Long, *The Witness of Preaching,* Westminster John Knox Press, 1989, p. 12.

3    See the excellent chapter 'The Life of Study' in Fred B. Craddock, *Preaching,* Abingdon Press, 1985, pp. 69–83.

4    See especially the excellent work by Leonora Tubbs Tisdale, *Preaching as Local Theology and Folk Art,* Fortress Press, 1997. Cf. David J. Schlafer, *What Makes This Day Different: Preaching Grace on Special Occasions,* Cowley Publications, 1992; Roger E. Van Harn, *Pew Rights: For people who listen to sermons,* Eerdmans, 1992; Mark Greene, *The Three-Eared Preacher*, London Bible College, 1998.

5    Van Harn, *Pew Rights,* pp. 155–8.

6    Here I am following especially Reginald R. Fuller, *What is Liturgical Preaching?*, SCM Press, 1957. Fuller's book seems now little known and is dated in several respects, but it provides a coherent rationale for different kinds of preaching in an Anglican setting. Cf. Ian Paton, 'Preaching and Worship', in Geoffrey Hunter, Gethin Thomas and Stephen Wright (eds), *A Preacher's Companion: Essays from the College of Preachers,* Bible Reading Fellowship, 2004, pp. 114–17. It was C. H. Dodd (*The Apostolic Preaching and its Developments,* Hodder & Stoughton, 1936, pp. 7–8) who made the distinction between 'proclamation', 'teaching' and 'exhortation' in the Early Church. Whether or not one can make quite such a clear distinction between these activities in the New Testament as Dodd suggests, it is useful to

distinguish them for practical purposes today. Fuller writes of the purpose of the sermon at the Eucharist as 'exhortation' (*paraklésis*), but for him such 'exhortation' is directly related to 'proclamation' (*kerygma*): it is the continued application of the gospel's medicine to people's lives.

7    Tim Stratford describes such an approach as especially suited to an urban context in his booklet *Interactive Preaching*, Grove Books, 1998: the 'preacher' offers some exegesis of a Scripture passage but invites the congregation to suggest ways in which it applies to their lives. Drama can also hugely enhance the act of proclamation.

8    On one level such rumours have become mere cliché, often based on endlessly repeated but little tested assertions about changing attention spans. However, there is academically serious work which argues that the sermon as we know it owes more to classical rhetoric than biblical warrant, and may fail to edify and equip congregations: see David C. Norrington, *To Preach or Not to Preach? The Church's Urgent Question*, Paternoster, 1996. But while 'teaching' certainly requires a variety of methods, the monologue as a vehicle for 'proclamation' can still, I believe, be authentic and effective.

9    Cf. the words from the service for the Ordination of Priests (*ASB*): 'You are to be messengers, watchmen, and stewards of the Lord; you are to teach and to admonish, to feed and to provide for the Lord's family, to search for his children in the wilderness of this world's temptations and to guide them through its confusions, so that they may be saved through Christ for ever.'

10    Clark, *Preaching in Context*, pp. 69–75, has an excellent discussion of the limits of 'application' in preaching.

11    For some ideas see Philip Tovey, *Preaching a Sermon Series with Common Worship*, Grove Books, 2004.

12    See especially Angela Butler, *Personality and Communicating the Gospel*, Grove Books, 1999; Malcolm Goldsmith and Martin Wharton, *Knowing Me, Knowing You*, SPCK, 1993.

# General index

*Note: Where more than one sequence of notes appears on the same page, reference to them is clarified by the addition of 'a', 'b' or 'c', thus 181 n.1c, 182 n.1b.*

# Index of biblical references